Practical Life-
Stress-less Financial Freedom

Your
Survival Guide
For Financial Success

What You Absolutely Positively Need to Know
(In Less than 200 Pages)

ISBN: 9798676863685

J. A. DOUGHERTY

MBA, CPA, RIA

Easy-to-understand Strategies for Investments, 401(k)s, Love Relationships, Home & Auto Buying, Wills & Trusts, Life Insurance and Other Financial Issues that Confound Us in Our Daily Lives.

www.DoughertyInvestments.com

Disclaimer

Table of Contents

Introduction

One of the reasons I started a career in financial planning was to better manage my own finances and to identify potential hidden traps that lay before me. Fortunately, I've designed this book so you don't have to make a career of financial planning. You only have to read the following pages and then refer to them later as needed.

During my years of helping clients plan their financial future, I've seen many books that go into detail—sometimes excruciating detail—about various concepts around this subject matter. But I don't think most of you want to read a 350-page book on tax planning or 15 chapters on how to optimize Social Security income.

I believe our society has made financial planning far too difficult and overly complex. Tax laws are a mess, estate planning is a blur—mostly because we die only once—and everyday things like home purchases and giving gifts to others are loaded with unintended minefields so that if we make a particular mistake we could end up spending—or losing—thousands more than we should.

Such challenges may come as the price for living in a society that strives to respect property rights, provides opportunities for advancement, governs by the rule of law, as well as allowing the freedom to make mistakes. But the price and complexity of it all is ever growing.

Meanwhile, a recent finding from a company called Bankrate.com reports that 45% of adult Americans do not have enough money to handle a thousand-dollar emergency. This includes things like an auto repair or an appliance breakdown. Most of us earn and spend week to week, paycheck to paycheck.

I have attempted to make each chapter an individual unit and to be written in as plain English as possible without confusing buzzwords and even fewer acronyms. The intent is that the reader can essentially get through the book during a two or three-hour commercial flight. Conversely, if you're not traveling much these days, you can put it by the bed stand or even in the bathroom next to the perennial joke book to leisurely bounce around from chapter to chapter as you wish.

Just as my office practice has come to address issues faced by young and old, what follows applies to multi-generations. So, when you're finished reading through the chapters and have worn out the cover, pass it on to other family members, especially the younger ones.

As for me, I have been helping clients in a financial planning and investment management practice for more than 30 years. You may think that having received an MBA from New York University and being accredited as a certified public accountant have provided me with enough credentials to write this book, but it's really all about the clients I have helped over the years and what I've learned from them. One sees just about everything at least once working with folks who are traveling through their financial life.

Upon writing my first book about managing couples' relationships, many of my friends were surprised that I had a foundation in such an area. What they may not realize is that even though our firm manages several million dollars of clients' hard-earned money, my profession is not about tabulating figures in a quiet corner. Similar to the proverbial bartender whose official job is to mix drinks, it is probably the most relationship intensive job one could have. In the course of helping clients, our firm is involved with all kinds of issues, including healthcare, family, love, marriage, divorce, death, bankruptcy, addictions, major purchases, and major losses. From time to time, there is even an opportunity to work on financial matters.

Yes, everything in our lives touches money. Someone once said that our entire life is consumed by making and settling debts. That's true whether we loan friends some money, pay a company in exchange for stock, or attend college because our parents have saved money for that purpose. It is what relationships are all about, too, whether I buy a pizza for some friends who help me move, or take my lover out for dinner after I said something stupid. The best planners, and I don't mean professional advisors, but everyday people, are those who realize that making debt and settling debt will lead to long-term success.

Many believe that the ultimate objective in managing and planning for their financial future is to reach a level of not just security, but overall freedom. The freedom to eventually do what they want, and when they want to, is a wonderful feeling that is hard to describe. Freedom from financial struggle, debt, and even freedom from the stress that comes with purchasing a house is what I want the reader to gain in managing their financial lives.

This book, however, does not attempt to touch every detail about money management. I'll leave intricate theories and fine print to my beloved professors who preside in towers of ivy and other vines. For example, I will not delve into every type of mutual fund fee structure nor will I include 50 pages explaining annuity terms, which is most likely beyond my ability, anyway. For this, the reader should be grateful.

As always, after reviewing a topic in the book, do not hesitate to investigate further your potential situation. The intention for what follows is to be an easy-to-read and understandable review of financial planning concepts with easy-to-apply strategies. For those with complicated situations, I highly recommend seeking the advice of a professional financial advisor or attorney. The wealthy already know this.

The other 45% borrow from their mother-in-law for that emergency auto repair.

Part One

INVESTING AND PLANNING FOR WEALTH ACCUMULATION

Chapter 1

First Things First: Saving Money *Without* Budgeting

Three Great Myths

1. Home budgets work for most people.
2. Most of us have income insufficient to allow for savings.
3. You can't save money without budgeting expenses.

I have already hinted at some of the statistics. Approximately 70% of Americans have less than $1,000 saved, and a recent survey indicate 45% have saved nothing. If the car breaks down, they must borrow from a relative, or use a payday check-cashing company, or simply leave the car stuck until they can scrape some cash together for the repair cost.

Perhaps ironically, most financial planning books contain detailed chapters about personal budgeting and tracking expenses. The theory goes that if you know what you're spending, you'll come up with the magical willpower to reduce it to start saving. To this I say, 'Hogwash!'

The same books also recommend establishing a three- to six-month emergency fund of savings, which is supposed to be separate from more permanent savings. It's hard to believe that someone who can't afford new tires is going to worry about setting aside perhaps $25,000 for a rainy day. Let's get real. If such budgeting and saving techniques were really effective, we would not have 70% of us with less than a thousand bucks in the bank.

This is not a book about debt management or paying off your credit cards, but we obviously have to be spending less than we're making in order to save, invest, and accumulate assets. Let's talk about *realistic* ways to do it.

A Scary Phrase: Credit Card Debt

Yes, scary, ugly, and downright depressing. When I had credit card debt, it made my whole outlook on life cloudy. If you're out of control with *your* credit cards, whereby you owe thousands and can barely make their minimum monthly payment, hire a credit counseling company to help you. If working with such a firm yields little results, resort to consulting a bankruptcy attorney. He or she can give you a legal structure and strategy to work toward a solution.

Going forward, throw away all of your credit cards, except one or two. Pay them off every month. If you can't manage this, then throw all away and just use a debit card. A debit card is not my first choice as I'll explain in Chapter 15, but at least with a debit card you can only spend what you have in the bank.

Try to pay your credit cards off, but don't wait until they are paid off to start saving. You may never get to this paid-off point.

Credit management experts advise that you pay the small credit card balances first, working up to the larger balances, one by one, often called snowballing. These initial small but positive steps provide a feeling of success and motivation.

In chapter three, I talk about Einstein's affection for compound interest. If Einstein was right about the positive effects of compound interest on savings, he was also right about the reverse: the negative consequences of compound interest on debt you owe. I can tell you firsthand how it accumulates and accumulates. I can also tell you the difference in mood and outlook and happiness when you get these debts paid off. It provides an amazing feeling of freedom and confidence.

You can't begin to realize significant effects from compound savings until you minimize the amount of your cash going toward credit card payments and their onerous interest charges.

Some experts also advise to pay off your debts before starting contributions to savings and retirement. Again, in the face of real-life situations, I disagree.

Saving Without Budgeting

The best way to save money is not to see it. Period. I have heard and read all of the books about household budgeting and watching your expenses and tracking them on different software applications, but none of them is as effective as not having the money you need to save *not* available to you in the first place.

How? We keep our allocated savings out of our grubby hands by having payroll deductions or automatic withdraws from our checking account. In these days of nifty banking technology it is very simple to do. But hardly any of us actually do. That is why we end up begging our mother-in-law to help us buy new tires.

Once you program automatic savings transfers from your payroll or checking account to a savings account, you will experience an almost euphoric feeling that you've accomplished the most important task: saving money for retirement. And, what's left in your checking account or paycheck is all yours to spend and enjoy. You can immediately escape feelings of guilt about passing through the years of your life without planning for a rainy day.

No Budgets Needed! Set it and Forget it.

Many financial gurus whom I respect but disagree with recommend initially saving for an emergency fund, rather than focusing on longer term investment and retirement plans. They suggest you have three to six months equivalent work income saved in a bank some place. The problem with this idea is that it's obviously not realistic for most of us to have the self-discipline to do this if we can't even buy new automobile tires. Can the average household bringing in, say, $80,000 per year manage to set aside $33,000 (5 months) of income? Wake-up financial gurus! Many savers get discouraged at this ambitious strategy and end-up saving nothing.

It is much more realistic—and productive—to focus on the long term now by getting money moved out of your reach before you find an excuse to spend it. Otherwise, you might hear yourself declaring, "Of course the Caribbean cruise was an emergency—my best friend was going, too!"

If you don't have a 401(k) or workplace pension plan to which to contribute, instruct your bank to withdraw a fixed amount each month from your checking account. View it as a monthly bill that has to be paid over which you have no control.

Your bank, any bank, can set up a monthly transfer whereby you elect, say, $50 per week, to be automatically transferred to an investment account. And remember, this investment account is not your Christmas fund or vacation plan. It's your long-term savings meant for your long-term life.

There are also new smart phone apps that allow you to seamlessly and automatically divert funds to savings and investment accounts, even very small amounts. Check out Square's Cash App; another is called Robinhood and still another is a company called Stockpile. Technology makes saving easier than ever. No excuses!

I also hear people complain that their income just isn't enough to allow savings. Those people need to get employment that pays more or find a second job. Part-time office work, clerking at a store, and janitoring are all classic second jobs. My stepfather was a school principal, but had five kids to support. He delivered pizza on the weekends for several years before a comfortable retirement in Florida.

401(k)s - Set it, and Forget it, Too

For those of you who have a 401(k) plan at work or similar savings plan, use these plans to do payroll deductions so that part of your wages systematically come out of your paycheck and go into your savings. Your contributions will often be supplemented by employer matching contributions, in essence, a free pay raise for you. To top it off, these contributions that you and your employer make are not subject to income tax.

The maximum amounts you may contribute to your workplace pension plan are significant. This year, 2020, the max is $19,500 for those under age 50, and $26,000 for those older.

But you don't have to do significant amounts, at least at first. Start off small. At first, ask your employer to withhold, say, 2% of your pay. You will see that somehow you survive. Then, after a year, increase that 2% up to 5%. It may take a bit of belt-tightening, but you'll see that it's doable. Look at it as something like tithing to your church, a similar worthy cause. I know several people who save 15% of their work income into their 401(k), an amount many planners say is the minimum we all should put away in order to have a comfortable retirement.

All of us think that we need to have available every dime we earn from work. But it's amazing, as adaptable beings, how we are able to get by with less. The opposite is also true. As we make more money, our spending magically keeps up and sometimes even exceeds what new funds we have.

What you don't see, you won't miss.

Make Sure Income Rises Faster than Lifestyle

I've known people who make a half million dollars per year who complain more about being broke than people who make $50,000. Why? The person who makes the half million dollars is usually a young professional experiencing this income level for the first time. And with this extra income he or she proceeds to go out and purchase three of the fanciest cars available, finds a big house with a big mortgage, and instead of taking one vacation per year, flies to Vegas every other month. What happened is that the lifestyle rose more quickly than the income. Meanwhile, the person making $50,000 a year drives around in an economy car that's 10 years old and takes a few trips to Florida every other year—and driving, not flying.

Yes, if you can't get your hands on your money, you can't spend it. My own situation is a case in point. During my first marriage it seemed like we were always financially struggling. Loan payments, college expenses, and eating out at nice restaurants constantly kept us strapped. After my divorce, I was faced with a large monthly marital support payment—for life. I thought for sure that I would end up in the poorhouse.

Strangely enough, since my divorce I have been able to save more money despite the alimony I have also had to pay. However, the really amazing thing I always think about is that if I were able to save and invest what I've paid in alimony over the years—again, money I don't really see—I would've been able to accumulate well over $2 million.

Perhaps we should look at saving for retirement as alimony—paid to ourselves for our own future.

The Amount Needed for Your Retirement

How much do we need to accumulate for retirement? We need enough saved so that we can go the rest of our lives drawing down on a combination of the principal we saved plus the income this principal generates. Numerous studies have been done to provide rules of thumb about how much we can take out of our savings and never have to worry about running out of money.

The most impressive study that I've seen tested investments over a 50-year period, testing investment portfolios through good and very bad times. The study found that withdrawing 6% annually from your savings in retirement will allow your money to last forever.

The biggest assumption is that you must invest your money with an allocation toward stocks as well as fixed income bonds. Obviously, if you simply put the savings under your mattress or into a 1% CD, 6% withdraws may not allow your retirement savings to last forever.

Let's put some numbers to this guideline. If you have accumulated $100,000 for retirement, you may withdraw $6,000 per year without fear of running out of money. On the other hand, if you have $1 million saved, you may safely withdraw $60,000 per year. The interesting thing is that the study revealed it doesn't matter when you start withdrawing this money. And why should it, if it will last forever?

I think the $1 million accumulated saving amount, as arbitrary and convenient as it may sound, is actually a good target for the average person. We already said that this amount will generate $60,000 annually. The median household income (3.1 people) in 2022 happened to be about $75,000. At retirement time, your social security income will be added to your other income, which will help approach and perhaps surpass the $75,000 figure. (I am not adjusting for inflation for future years because as inflation occurs, your wages and your savings will also inflate in tandem. In other words, there is enough to worry about without having to get bogged down with hypothetical inflation rate assumptions, which no one seems to be able to predict, anyway.)

Don't fret that you'll never be able to put away $1 million. You won't have to. That's where compound interest comes in. And the secrets of compound interest are explained in the next chapter.

No Excuses: You Get to Enjoy 95% Now

As I've worked with clients over many years, I have found it curious why some people tend to be excellent savers and others are just plain lousy. Perhaps the better savers have a built-in optimism about the future, and others believe there's so little promise in what the future holds, saving for it is futile. In other words, it is the view that, *if I have money today, I'm going to spend it today and live for today, because I can't trust what tomorrow will bring.*

Look in the mirror and honestly ask yourself which category of person you are. If you find that you may be a spend-it-all-now type, force yourself to compromise. I'm only asking you to initially put aside about 5% of your income; you get to enjoy the rest now. Statistically, if you are age 25, there is a 9 out of 10 chance that you will make it to age 60. So don't fool yourself by thinking that with all the beer you drink and ex-wives you have, you won't make it to old age—you probably will. That's why you'll need a nest egg of savings.

Three Critical Takeaways from Chapter

1. Having money saved adds to happiness and reduces stress.
2. You don't have to budget to save.
3. Saving even 5% of your income starts a bright future.

Chapter 2

Einstein was Right About Investing Too

Three Great Myths

1. CDs are the safest investment.
2. Stocks are a risky investment.
3. Saving a few dollars now rather than later won't make much difference, especially because I may not even survive to old age.

In the previous chapter we talked about accumulating $1 million in savings to allow withdrawals of $60,000 annually—forever. If that idea isn't fantastic enough, there's something else about this plan that's even better:

We don't have to save $1 million to get $1 million. Instead, we only have to save a fraction of this amount, invest it wisely, and allow time to do its magic.

Albert Einstein is supposed to have remarked that a force in nature even stronger than gravity is the power of compound interest, reported to have called it the eighth wonder of the world.

With a 1% annual rate of return, did you know that it will take about 72 years for your money to double in value? But, and here's where Einstein comes in, if you can get just three percentage points more, that is, 4% per year, your money will double in only 18 years. And double again in the next 18 years.

The words of Einstein are never truer as we watch the prolonged results of earning what can only be described as chronically paltry CD interest rates. Since the crash of 2008, and our latest temporary inflation bump, bank savings rates have tumbled down and have not gotten back up. At this writing, the average one-year bank CD pays about 1.8% annual interest.

And more "good" news to add insult to injury: CD income is subject to income tax, which further reduces its growth. Ouch!

Let's take a look at real numbers. A $10,000 CD earning 1% grows to just $11,961 after <u>18 years</u>. Yes, my math is correct. However, the same $10,000 earning 4% will have more than doubled, reaching $20,258.

Now you can see that it is not necessary to save a million bucks to accumulate a million bucks.

For some of my older readers, I know what you may be saying: *John, I'm not planning to be around 18 years from now, so what do I care? And anyway, interest rates are going to return soon to where they were in the good old days.*

First, even if you leave this earth anytime soon, or not so soon, most of your money will still be here, to be inherited by your heirs. So, it's not just *your* life span we are talking about, but the life span of your *children and grandchildren.* With this thought, we could be talking about a duration of 50 years or more.

Second, with regard to interest rates bouncing back, consider Japan's plight. That country has had low interest rates for 25 years now. The United States is only—only?—in its twelfth year of very low rates. About seven years ago, experts confidently proclaimed that our country is different from Japan, and as such, we will not experience the same economic slow-growth funk in which Japan finds itself. After all, Japan is a country that has an aging population, large government debt, and growing social programs.

Whoops—does that sound familiar? Could Japan's situation, as well as slow growth around the world, portend low interest rates for some time to come for us, too?

The solution to the dilemma: Add diversification into your savings with securities that pay better income and have a chance to grow more than the $20 bills stuffed under your mattress. Consider some corporate and municipal bonds, which, though not guaranteed by the federal government, are guaranteed by the issuer and mature to a fixed date with a fixed principal like a CD.

Also consider blue chip stocks that happen to pay good income. Did you know that Verizon stock, though its principal is not guaranteed, pays an income rate of more than 4%, and that ATT pays more than 5% annual income? Even good old Duke Energy pays an annual income rate of about 4%.

Remember, 4% may not sound much different than 1%, but over the years, the effect of compound growth will make a huge difference. We'll learn more about investing in Chapter 4 so we can receive returns of even more than 4%.

Don't Buy Paper Towels at 7-11 and Don't Do All Your Investing with CDs

Do you realize that investing is like buying paper towels? Should we buy paper towels at the very convenient corner gas station, or should we make a little extra effort by driving a few more miles down the road to the big supermarket?

Clearly, what's convenient may not always be the best deal. And with investments, that's especially true in this era of low interest rates, in which typical CD rates are less than one percent.

First, to understand why rates may stay low for some time to come, let's take a look at the major economic trends driving things out there.

<u>Demographics, Demographics, Demographics.</u> If real estate is about location, location, location, the economy in this era is about

demographics, demographics, demographics. Slowing and aging population trends are driving a slow-growth picture, not only for the U.S., but for all of the developed world.

Let's follow stock market performance backwards: Stocks increase in value because company profits increase. Company profits increase when their sales go up; sales go up primarily because there are more customers, and these customers are able to spend more money.

Population trends, however, point toward a spending pace whose growth is not sufficient to bring out the party hats anytime soon.

Historically, the U.S. has averaged over 3% annual growth in its economy, and even more when rebounding out of a recession. But not over the last several years. We're lucky to hit 2%. To spur growth, the Federal Reserve has kept short term interest rates low for banks, and unfortunately, the banks pass these near-zero rates on to customers in the form of terrible CD rates.

Alternatives to Shopping at 7-11

Stocks: Historically, stocks average 10-12% growth per year. In the long-term, investors who have bet on the economy by investing in stocks, have won. Even if the 10-12% drops by half to a 5% average, that is still particularly good in this era of crummy income yields.

Besides growth, many stocks pay good annual dividend income. Yes, investors typically look to have two components of profit from owning a stock: one, its increase in value, and two, the annual dividend that companies pay to its shareholders. Each company is different in this growth vs. income profile.

Amazon stock, for instance, pays no annual dividend, but its stock price has increased significantly in value. ATT, on the other hand, pays an annual income dividend of over 5%, but the value of the stock has not increased much in recent times.

Growing at an annual rate of 10%, the stock market's historical growth rate, will double your savings in about eight years. Using this arithmetic, your savings could triple in 24 years. Billionaire Warren Buffett invests primarily in stocks.

Bonds: Historically, bonds average less growth than stocks, but typically pay more annual income and have less volatility risk than stocks. Why? Because bonds come with a contractual guarantee from the issuer to pay the principal back and to pay, usually, a stated interest rate. Only if the issuer of the bond goes bankrupt can the terms change. Fortunately, it's not difficult to find good corporate and government bonds that significantly exceed the income paid by bank CDs.

A bond paying even 3% interest per year will double in about 24 years—not as fast as the average stock will, but still much better than the more than 72 years it takes for a CD to double in value.

Your savings need to include stocks and bonds so that you can optimally take advantage of compound growth principles. You can do this with your 401(k), an IRA, or a non-retirement savings account. We'll discuss these options in chapters 5 and 6.

Make Time Your Friend

As I describe savings balances magically doubling and tripling as a result of compound growth, the second component, besides the annual rate of growth, is obvious: time. The more time we can allow our investments to grow, the more compound growth magic we witness. That is why every financial planning book ever written extols the wonderful benefits of starting to invest sooner rather than later. The person who begins to save at age 25 will see much more magic than he or she who starts at 50.

To illustrate, one who saves $5,000 per year, starts at age 18, and earns average investment returns, will have only contributed $200,000, but savings will have grown to more than $1.1 million by age 58.

On the other hand, if I started saving $5,000 per year at age 40, my accumulation at age 58 would only be about $270,000.

The Power of Time and Savings

	ANNUAL AMOUNT SAVED		
	$10,000	$15,000	$20,000
	ACCUMULATED MASS OVER TIME		
5 years	$63,359	$95,039	$126,718
10 years	$156,455	$234,683	$312,910
15 years	$293,243	$439,865	$586,486
20 years	$494,229	$741,344	$988,458
25 years	$789,544	$1,184,316	$1,579,088
30 years	$1,223,459	$1,835,189	$2,446,918

As you can see from the chart above, the earlier you start saving the better. The first column shows that if you can put away $10,000 per year for 30 years, you have contributed $300,000, but through the power of compounding and stock market growth, your account would have grown to $1,223,459. However, if you started just 10 years later and save for 20 years, accumulated savings is only $494,229, 60% less. That's a huge difference.

I can only smile when clients recount the story about their Uncle Henry or Aunt Mary who drove an old Chevy and lived in a small modest house. Upon their deaths, usually around age 90, the heirs discover that Uncle Henry was worth $3 million. They were surprised, but I was not. He invested in stocks and he did it for a long time.

By the way, billionaire investor Warren Buffett is age 93 at this writing and is the 3rd richest person in the world. More about Mr. Buffet in Chapter 3.

It looks like Einstein was right—again.

Three Critical Takeaways from Chapter

1. Time is your friend; take advantage of it to start saving now.
2. Accumulated compound growth is magic if annual growth rates are decent; it's lousy if all your money is in a CD.
3. You'll live longer than you think, and your invested money can take advantage of that long life.

Chapter 3

Why Warren Buffet Became a Millionaire, and You Can Too

Three Great Myths:

1. If you're not an investing genius like Buffet, you can't make any money.
2. He knows when to get in and out of the market.
3. Buffet analyzes the stock market very closely.

When writing a book about financial planning and investing, it's sort of hard to avoid at least mentioning Warren Buffett. As the third richest man in the world and it's most successful investor, it is difficult to not have at least one chapter highlighting his philosophy and methods so we can learn from the master.

Many of us know that his estimated personal worth is about $88 billion, that he's lived in the same house in Omaha Nebraska since 1958, and that he drives himself to work every day. Some other Buffet aficionados may also be aware that he stops at a local McDonald's on his way to work every day for the same breakfast and, that during the course of the day, he drinks several diet and cherry Coca-Colas.

Now that we know what he eats for breakfast, do we really understand what his investment philosophy has been that has brought all of the success? To watch cable business shows give daily reports on the markets, I would say no.

The Jim Cramer Method

When we watch the stock market cable shows, including *Mad Money* with Jim Cramer, he constantly harps on economic trends and short-term stock price movements. Cramer and his colleagues love to create news by announcing hikes in the federal reserve rate or the likelihood of a recession in Europe.

I have some friends who pay large fees to national brokerage companies for a portfolio management program. Invariably, these management programs buy and sell stocks like crazy based on computer algorithms that indicate when it's time to buy and sell during certain periods and trends. Many of their clients are impressed with all of the account activity.

The only problem: The most successful investor in the world, Warren Buffett, ignores all of those principles.

Instead, the most successful investor in the world does not care about stock price trends or the world economy. Instead, he focuses on—no, laser focuses on—the companies themselves in which he invests. Buffett claims that he doesn't buy stocks, he buys ownership of companies.

What's more, Warren Buffett buys the stocks of companies that he believes will be successful over many years, not just this week or next month. And he doesn't buy CD's or mutual funds. "If I had listened to economic forecasts, I would never have made any money."

Traditional Investment Allocation Theory

One of the topics I cover in the next chapter relates to the different types of investments and the choices we have, including stocks, funds, bonds, and mutual funds. A first step for all investors should be to determine how much of your portfolio you want exposed to growth assets, like stocks, as opposed to so-called fixed assets, like CD's, bonds and bond funds.

The traditional theory is that you reduce the volatility in a portfolio by having fixed income securities mixed in with your stocks. Academic studies have shown that if you have approximately 60% allocated to stocks and 40% to fixed income, you'll find the perfect balance between growth and stability. It's been called the efficient frontier.

Some clients want no stocks at all and instead prefer to have all fixed income assets, such as bonds and perhaps preferred stock. They feel more secure in knowing that if the stock market drops 20% or 30%, their portfolio will be stable. It's a personal choice and a personal decision, but one that must be addressed when you're creating an investment plan for yourself. In my office, I have developed a risk tolerance test with hypothetical questions that attempt to measure a client's nervousness about stock market fluctuations: the more nervous, the fewer stocks and the more fixed income, such as bond holdings, positions.

Buffett Allocation Theory

However, if you're a long-term investor, Buffett says hogwash. When asked about bond investing, he has responded more than once, *Why should I put money into bonds when they earn only about half of what stocks do in the long term*? He comfortably and nonchalantly ignores the volatility of a portfolio that invests solely in stocks. Most of my clients would be very nervous if they had a 100% stock portfolio as they watch daily reports about impending economic crises.

The most successful client in our firm is a couple who has invested all their money entirely in stocks. Not stock *funds*, not annuities, and not bonds, but 100% individual common stocks and less than 15 in number. Over the years, stock selections have been adjusted but the strategy has been essentially one of buy-and-hold blue chip company stocks while ignoring day-to-day and even year-to-year stock market fluctuations. Their portfolio has grown to many millions of dollars. When I remind the clients that a mere drop of two percent in the stock market means a loss of several hundred thousand dollars, they shrug their shoulders and respond, "But it will go back up eventually."

And it always has—over the long term.

A stock fund or exchange traded fund is a bucket of stocks. We'll discuss different types of funds in chapter five. The fund bucket may hold a category or sector of stocks, such as utility stocks. Or it may hold a broad collection of varied industries, such as the familiar S&P 500 fund, which is a collection of the supposed largest 500 companies spread across all sectors. If the stocks in the fund are selected by hired stock-picker experts, then it is called a managed fund. If, on the other hand, the stocks in the fund are picked randomly with the goal of representing an entire sector, the fund is called an index fund.

Warren Buffett does not typically invest in funds, managed or index. Instead, his company, Berkshire Hathaway, studies the fundamental performance, leadership, and long-term potential of individual corporations that promise success into the future. Because he invests in various companies over several years, he is able to care much less about day-to-day stock price movements and the endless news chatter we read and hear.

Having said that Buffett does not invest in funds, it is perhaps ironic that Berkshire Hathaway is itself a fund. Investors that have stuck with Berkshire over the years have profited greatly. Currently, the per share price of Berkshire Hathaway is more than $300,000. That's the price of just one share!

Even though Buffett avoids investment funds, and he often pooh-poohs them for other investors, he acknowledges that many of us, especially small investors, nonetheless, should use funds as investment vehicles, especially those that don't trust themselves or other investment advisors to study and manage stock portfolios. Buffet's Berkshire Hathaway fund has had difficulty outperforming the S&P 500 index fund lately, perhaps because his asset pool is so large. It is almost like a mini S&P index in itself.

Proof is in the Chart

Chart: The Power of Compound Growth; The Power of Stock Growth Over Time

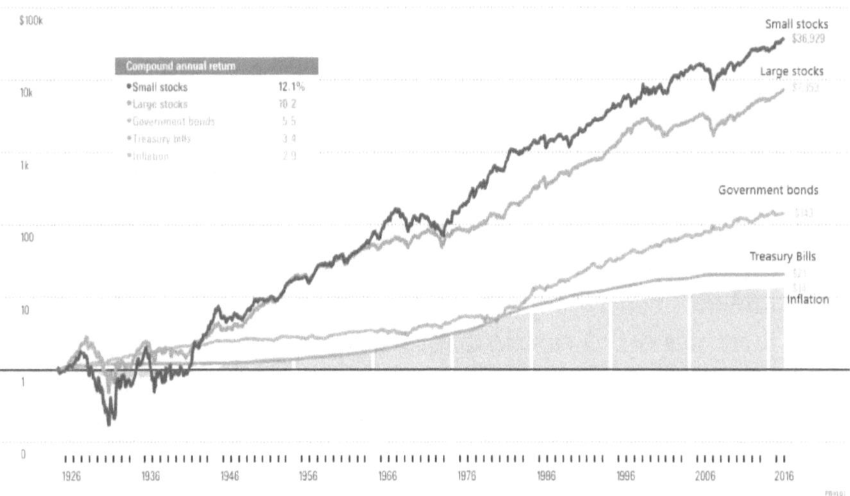

The above chart of stock and bond performance is certainly a picture worth a thousand words. At least it shows what has happened to one dollar invested as it has compounded over time. You can see that a dollar invested in 1926 in large corporate stocks has grown to a value of $7,353 by the year 2017. Amazing growth. In contrast, a dollar invested in bonds has grown to $143. The multiple for which bonds have grown is impressive as they've averaged annually 5.5%, but its growth is left in the dust by stock performance.

The fascinating thing about this chart is that it is so easy to forget all of the historical dramas and traumas that the market has persevered through. During the time exhibited on the chart our country has suffered through a devastating depression, a life-changing world war, a Cold War, cultural upheaval in the 60s, a major energy crisis, good and bad presidents, and on and on. Still, all of these major events appear as little blips on the relentless rise of the stock market.

As we travel through time with the graph climbing, we see the impact of the stock market's 10.2% average annual return and how it completely dwarfs the graph of the bond returns. Einstein's compound growth principle is illustrated with over-whelming evidence here.

We may ask ourselves how such a phenomenon of continuing stock price appreciation can happen with all of these intervening events in history. I believe the answer is twofold. First, our economic system and culture allow individuals to have the freedom to discover new businesses and to make them successful. I also believe that given this freedom, workers in our companies have a strong desire to work hard and create success.

When you think of it, we really do live in an amazing society in which an average person can sit back, buy a few shares of Apple Corporation, and have confidence that society will create an environment of success for that company and that its employees will work their tails off to ensure that success.

A major challenge that we have as stockholders is often finding the courage to buy into the stock market and then stay in during tough times. Many people leave thousands of dollars sitting idly on the sidelines because they are waiting for "the right time" to buy. Many others panic in a down market, sell their stock positions and delay getting back in. Then they complain that they tried stocks but it was a lousy experience. If you suffer from procrastination or from nervous feet, you probably need an advisor who can hold your hand, implement an action plan, and at times, walk you off the ledge.

Whether you are just starting out in a new job, out of school, or reviewing how you pass down a portfolio to heirs, your portfolio must include stocks or stock funds. Uncle Warren would insist on it.

Quotes of Warren Buffett:

- *If you buy me a glass of wine now, I'll drink it and it will be gone. On the other hand, if you give me the $5 that the wine costs, and I can invest it, in 10 years the $5 turns into $12.*
- *The modern portfolio theory of blind diversification (index funds) will allow you to do average in the long run. But I think anyone can figure out how to do average by the fifth grade.*
- *The size of the investor's brain is less important than the ability to detach the brain from the emotions.*
- *After I buy a stock, I would not be disturbed if stock markets closed for a year or two. I don't need a daily quote to validate the well-being of my investment.*

- *If you aren't willing to own a stock for 10 years, don't even think about owning it for 10 minutes.*
- *In the short-term, the market is a popularity contest; in the long term it is a weighing machine.*
- *When investing, we view ourselves (at Berkshire) as business analysts, not as market, economic, or security analysts.*
- *When the price of a stock can be influenced by a 'herd' on Wall Street with prices set at the margin by the most emotional person or the greediest person, or the most depressed person, it is hard to argue that the market always prices rationally. In fact, market prices are frequently nonsensical.* (The reaction of the markets to the recent pandemic is a good example.)
- *The pain of loss is far greater than the enjoyment of a gain. This aversion to loss makes investors unduly conservative.*
- *In the short run, investor sentiment—human emotion—has a more pronounced impact on stock prices than a company's fundamentals.*
- *The increase in short-term stock trading over the last 50 years has worked to widen the price-to-value gap, increase the noise in the markets, and lead to spikes in volatility. In this world, an investor who is hostage to short-term performance pressures will feel nothing but discontent.*
- *The time to buy stocks is when there is blood on the street.*

Three Critical Takeaways from Chapter

1. Every long-term investor needs to own some stocks and or stock funds.
2. Turn the daily stock market reports off—they'll just drive you crazy.
3. If company and fund analysis is not your thing, hire a financial advisor, especially if a lack of knowledge, time, or confidence lends to procrastination.

Part Two

NUTS AND BOLTS OF INVESTMENT MANAGEMENT

Chapter 4

The Lingo of Stocks, Funds, and Other Strange Things

Three Great Myths

1. All mutual funds are the same.
2. An IRA is a specific investment.
3. An index fund is evenly allocated among its securities in the fund.

Let's define in simple terms what our alphabet soup of financial instruments is. And by the way, the terms financial instruments, securities, and financial investments all mean pretty much the same thing. I'll also provide some tips and advice along the way.

Most investors have some combination of the investments described below. It is important to understand these terms because not knowing will allow you to succumb to ignorant investing strategies, possibly pay higher fees, and experience lower investment returns, which over several years, could be the difference between being able to take a decent vacation once in a while and not being able to afford to get your teeth fixed.

Bank Savings and Money Market Accounts—A convenient place to keep temporary limited amounts of money. Usually these deposits are insured up to $250,000 (and maybe more if you have multiple accounts titled in various ways, like one individually and another jointly) by the federal government agency FDIC (Federal Deposit Insurance Corporation).

Funds can usually be withdrawn at any time without penalty and often come with checks you can use, but current interest rates earned on these accounts are terribly low—usually less than a half percent per year. Remember chapter three about buying paper towels at a convenience store.

Bank CDs—They really aren't certificates of deposit anymore, but that's what the banks still call them, probably to make them sound more important, and to justify their penalties if you cash in before their maturity (completion) date. If you cash in early, you don't lose principal, but a portion or all of your earned interest, which is probably not significant these days. Like bank savings accounts, CDs are FDIC insured, and like other bank savings accounts, pay relatively low interest rates. In 2020 they average about 1% for a two-year term.

These low interest rates over time, say 20 years, are murder on the growth of your money. You really have to be careful how you define "safe," when it comes to investments. A lack of volatility in value over the short term sounds comfortable, but often means lower returns that may not even keep pace with normal inflation over time.

For that part of your portfolio where you still may want a bank CD, say, because you need money in six months for a house down payment, shop around online, but keep it simple. If they advertise options you don't understand, stay away. Yes, CDs are in the convenience store paper towel category, too.

Stocks—Also called common stocks or equity. When you own a stock, you are also "long"—as opposed to short (see what selling short means below) in a stock. As an owner of common stock, you are part owner of the company in which you hold the stock. When stockholders vote on corporate issues, such as proposed mergers or board of directors, you'll get a vote, too. Fun.

But here's what's not so fun: As a shareholder, you receive no guarantees from the company to get your original investment amount back—not tomorrow or next year or anytime. You just hope that when you're ready to sell, there's some eager buyer out there in the stock marketplace willing to pay more for your shares than you did. In that respect, owning stock is a lot like owning real estate.

But better than most real estate investments, the company whose stock you own may distribute part of its profits to you every year, called dividends. Different companies pay different dividend amounts. AT&T pays a whopping dividend that's equivalent to about

5% of its share price. Alphabet Inc. (that's the official name for the Google empire), on the other hand, pays no dividend. Zero, zilch. But guess which stock has risen more in the last several years: Alphabet. Why? The market believes that AT&T will not grow as quickly as Alphabet/Google. Google tells its shareholders they don't want to distribute any of the profits because they have creative ways to use the money internally so the company can continue significant growth. So far, Alphabet shareholders believe this.

Interestingly, many studies show that in the long-term dividend-paying stocks do better than those which do not pay dividends.

Warren Buffett says that money intended to be invested for more than a few years, should be heavily in stocks. Who's to argue with him? Stocks have averaged 10% growth per year over the last 100 years.

<u>The Dow Jones 30 and S&P 500</u>—We hear it every day on the news: the Dow rose 50 points, or the S&P went down a half a percent. Most people I talk to, however, have no idea what the Dow and the S&P are. You will now.

Each index is a bucket of stocks selected to represent the entire stock market. The stocks that are selected for each of these buckets are picked by companies that do business on Wall Street: the Dow Jones Company (which also produces The Wall Street Journal newspaper) selects the Dow 30 and Standard and Poor's Financial Services, LLC., determines the S&P 500 stocks. The managers of these companies hope that stocks they select for their list will be representative of the thousands and thousands of stocks that are bought and sold in the stock market. By following these sample groups, we hope to gauge how well stocks are doing as an entire group.

For instance, the Dow list of stocks consists of what we would normally call blue chippers. That is, stocks of companies that are well-established and stable. At this printing, the 30 companies are:

American Express
Amgen
Apple
Boeing
Caterpillar

Chevron
Cisco
Coca-Cola
Dow
Goldman Sachs
Home Depot
Honeywell
IBM
Intel
Johnson & Johnson
JP Morgan Chase
McDonalds
Merck
Microsoft
Nike
Proctor & Gamble
Salesforce.com
Travelers Insurance
United Health Group
Verizon
Visa
Walgreens Boots Alliance
Walmart
Walt Disney
3M

As you can see, they are all huge, successful companies and from various industries. Once a company finds itself on the list it is not guaranteed to stay there forever. It was big news when GE (General Electric) was dropped from the list after several years of very poor performance. Yes, over time the Dow Jones index is slanted toward successful companies, so in reality it may not be an accurate long-term gauge of total stock market performance.

Another problem with the Dow index is that there are only 30 companies on the list. Can 30 companies adequately measure the performance of the entire stock market? That is where the S&P 500 index comes in, as a list of not 30 but 500—supposedly largest—companies whose stocks trade on the New York Stock Exchange or the NASDAQ. Many believe this is a better gauge of overall stock market performance because it is a bigger bucket.

There are many lists that Wall Street firms track to measure stock market performance including the Russell 2000 and the NASDAQ index. Obviously, the Russell 2000 is even a bigger sample size bucket than the S&P 500 and includes companies of smaller size. The NASDAQ index has become synonymous with the tech company index because many of the new tech companies are traded on this exchange.

Bonds—The same idea as a CD, but instead of lending money to a bank, we're lending money to the organization issuing the bond. They are the borrower-issuer, whether a corporation, a charitable entity, or a local, state, federal, or foreign government.

Unlike shareholders, but similar to CD owners, bondholders receive a contractual guarantee from the issuer that they'll receive their principal back at the end of stated term plus interest income. However, unlike FDIC insured CD's, bonds are not insured by the federal government unless the federal government actually issues the bonds.

The rates that bonds pay are in large part based on the degree of risk or likelihood that the bond issuer will not meet its guaranteed promise to refund the principal at the end of the term. It's dangerous to give an average rate, but in the past, a lower risk bond might pay something like 3% for a 10-year term, while a risky bond with the same length maturity could pay 6% or more. These high-risk bonds are often termed junk bonds.

For example, bond buyers like you and me (that is, those who are *lending* money to the bond issuers) believe strongly that Apple Corporation will be able to honor its promise to pay back principal in the future, and as a result, interest rates on Apple bonds are quite low.

On the other hand, buyers of Tesla bonds demand a higher interest rate because the automaker struggles financially and is more likely to default on its legal repayment promise.

After bonds are initially issued to lenders, the lenders can usually sell their bonds to other buyers on the secondary bond market.

Interim prices for bonds on the secondary market may vary depending on the quality of the borrower-issuer. The secondary price may also vary if market interest rates change. If rates in the general market rise, the existing bond's "old" lower rate is relatively less attractive than those of new bonds, so the interim value of the old bond drops. Note, however, that even if the interim market value changes, the bond still matures at its predetermined contract value, call *par value.*

The interim market price of an existing bond will also change if its issuer appears to become increasingly more or less risky, such as a pending bankruptcy. When the city of Detroit entered bankruptcy a few years ago, its bonds dropped in price significantly, and indeed, dropped the interim market price of many bonds issued by municipalities. Most have since recovered.

In general, however, bond market prices are much more stable than stocks, and if you hold until they mature, again, they always return to their par value. This aspect is always missing when business news headlines ominously announce that "bond prices are falling," or, "It's not a good time to buy bonds." These blurbs are nonsense if the owner of a bond simply holds on until it matures—to its contracted principal value.

Although Warren Buffett will disagree because of the historically lower growth that bonds provide compared to stocks, investors who want to avoid the price volatility of stocks may opt for bonds for part or all of their securities investments.

Preferred Stock—There's lots of confusion with this one. I think the easiest way to think about a preferred stock is to look at it as a hybrid between stock and bond characteristics. Preferred stock is issued by corporations looking to receive funds. Like a bond, preferreds pay good income and typically don't change much in value. But like a stock, there are no contractual guarantees of income or principal, and there is usually no maturity date. That's why preferred stocks usually pay a higher rate of income than bonds.

Also, like common stock, preferred stock income paid to investors is called dividends, but unlike common stock, under current tax law, preferred stock dividends do not receive lower tax rates like common stock.

Preferred stocks have the place in a portfolio designed for income and relative stability. Often, retired investors like preferred for that reason, willing to give up the potential for much growth in exchange for a nice dividend check.

Yes, prices of preferred stock are less volatile than those of common stock, but it doesn't mean you won't see scary times. During the 2008 stock crash, preferred tumbled, too, particularly those issued by banks. Most have nicely recovered since.

Like bonds, the market price of a preferred stock moves inversely to interest rate changes: As interest rates in the economy rise, existing preferred stock prices usually fall. This will happen frequently over the course of ownership and be a large part of the reason for intermittent volatility. When it happens, don't panic!

Mutual Funds - People ask me all the time: *John, do you think a mutual fund is a good investment?"*

The implication in their question, of course, is that there is only one mutual fund or one type of mutual fund. Just the opposite is true. There are almost as many funds and fund investment styles as there are stars in the sky.

Let's start with the very basics. A mutual fund is a bucket that holds several securities in which individual investors own a partial collective share. If the overall bucket does well, all the individual investors' value increases as well. And vice versa.

The most basic thing to know is that not all funds put the same type of investments in their bucket. Funds vary by investment objective. One fund may put all common stock in its bucket, another all bonds, and another a mixture of different stocks, bonds, and other securities. Some funds only have stocks of high-tech companies, or perhaps only utility companies, or maybe just utility companies in China.

Funds are managed by companies that have names that are familiar to many of us, such as Fidelity or Vanguard. These big boys just don't manage one fund but many different funds so that they can meet different investment objectives or targets of their investing customers.

The most well-known fund is one that simply includes in its bucket the 500 largest companies on a list compiled by a staff of people at a company called Standard and Poor's. If these 500 companies' stocks do well collectively, investors investing in this fund do well. Historically over the long term, it's done very well. Many fund manager companies, including the two just mentioned, offer such a fund, called the S&P 500 fund. Investing in such a fund has become the most popular way for people like us to participate in the stock market

Think of it—by investing simply in an S&P 500 mutual fund, you can be indirectly part owner—that is, shareholder—in companies like Microsoft, Alphabet (Google), and even McDonalds. What a country!

Besides different types of securities that a fund may have in its bucket, the other two important ways that funds differ from each other are 1) how they determine which securities within their class to put into the bucket, and 2) how they charge their customers—investors like us who buy a piece of the bucket.

1. How funds determine which securities to put into bucket. Fund managers typically use one of two strategies to choose which securities to put into their bucket: The first strategy involves some type of analysis by so-called experts trying to choose the best securities in the fund's class. So, if the theme of the fund is utility companies, the fund managers carefully evaluate and then buy what they believe to be the best utility companies to put into the bucket for their customers. They also decide to sell stocks in the fund based on the same analysis. These funds are typically called *managed funds.*

   The other strategy for deciding which securities to put into a given fund is really no strategy at all: Simply go out and find those securities of companies that usually meet a size requirement and dump them into the bucket. The aforementioned S&P 500 fund is a perfect example. No expert analyzes the quality of the individual companies; the fund simply includes those stocks of companies that match a certain size, usually by revenue. There is no Harvard genius—or investment guru like Warren Buffett— trying to pick winners and avoid losers. This type of passive selection process is often called "index fund" management. It's also simply called passive investing.

Various mutual fund management companies, such as Vanguard, maintain such index funds, and most companies create funds for various sectors, too. As a result, we can buy a passive fund made up of just technology company stocks or bonds of European countries. Yes, such funds can participate in stock, bond, preferred stock, and even real estate stocks (often called Real Estate Investment Trusts or REITs). Therefore, if you don't have faith in the experts picking the right bio pharmaceuticals, but you know it is a sector in which you want to invest, just look for an index fund that specializes in such securities.

Wait a minute—Does this sound sort of scary, investing in a list of companies without knowing the stars from the duds? Don't we need hot shot analysts to create a managed fund to insure superior performance? Well, as it turns out, studies show that index passive funds usually outperform those actively managed. Can you believe it? Believe it. As it turns out, managed funds too often make the same mistakes that Buffett warns us about: too much buying and selling in attempts to find optimum periods to trade, not enough fundamental analysis of the company's stock they're buying, and not having the patience to hold on when they happen to find such a company.

Another consequence of all of the buying and selling in managed funds: a bigger tax bill for you. That's right, a fund that is managed has greater turnover and as it sells stocks owned by the fund with gains, these gains must be passed on to owners of the fund. Such passed-on-profits are called capital gains distributions. Every tax season I hear complaints from managed mutual funds owners about paying capital gains taxes though they haven't sold anything. Contrast this to index funds made up of a list of securities that are not actively traded. Such funds produce much fewer capital gains distributions and in the industry are therefore termed *tax efficient*.

In addition, as you might have guessed, guru hotshot fund managers charge more to run managed funds. You probably figured out by now that higher fees eat into investment performance.

2. How funds charge their customers. Funds normally charge an annual fee, deducted straight from the fund.

   Some funds get a little more clever and charge an additional fee when you initially buy into the fund—so called Class A funds. That's called a front loaded or front-end fee. Still other funds get even more clever and charge a back-end load whereby an extra fee is charged when you *sell* the fund—called, you guessed it, a class B type fund. Most back-end funds have a fee that declines annually, usually reaching zero by the end of the fifth year.

Tip: Avoid mutual funds that have back or front-end loaded fees. I assure you that comparable funds are available to purchase without such costs. Often, your friendly advisor (perhaps a cousin who just acquired his brokerage license) will sell you a loaded fund, which is how he receives initial and ongoing commissions.

To repeat, most funds, including loaded funds, also charge annual fees because even index funds require staff and overhead to operate. Managed funds (with guru stock pickers) typically charge more than passive index funds. These days you can get a top-rated managed fund that charges around 1% annually; you can easily find top-rated index funds charging less than 0.25%.

Morningstar Rating - Morningstar is an independent company out of Chicago formed many years ago with the goal of objectively evaluating mutual funds, then summing up the fund with a handy rating from one to five stars, five being very superior in its class, and one star, a pathetic dog. The rating considers much more than just periodic performance. It compares a fund to others in its class and investment objective, taking into account things like fees, manager profiles, and dividend payouts.

Morningstar's ratings were a bit more useful years ago when there weren't so many funds and differences were more pronounced. Still, if a fund is a one star, run, and run pretty quickly from it. I usually like to stay with just four and fivers, but from time to time will find a three-star fund that I like. To find ratings, visit web sites such as Google Finance or Yahoo Finance. Big fund management company sites, such as that of Vanguard, may also include independent ratings—especially if they happen to be awarded lots of stars.

Target Retirement funds - I promise to be done with mutual funds in a few minutes, but each year Wall Street invents new versions which need some explanation. One of these new—and perhaps not so new now—fangled types of funds are commonly referred to as target funds. These buckets usually comprise a variety of stocks and bonds, based on the primary theory that investors always need a portion of each (as opposed to Warren Buffett's practice of owning virtually all stocks). The secondary theory of target funds is that as we get older, we need to become more conservative, driving us to own a smaller portion of stocks in favor of more and more bonds.

The idea behind a target retirement fund is that each is designed with an identified specific date you retire. The further into the future, the higher allocation of stocks in the fund. Thus, the Vanguard Target Retirement 2050 Fund has a larger proportion of stocks and fewer bonds than the similar Target Retirement 2025 Fund, providing the older person who plans to retire in about five years less volatility and risk than a younger person set to retire 30 years from now.

I only half-heartedly recommend target funds. The major problem in this era of longer life: Even the 65-year-old new retiree has a good chance of making it to 90, especially one of a married couple, which puts us back to a long, not short, term period. The investment period is even longer if you consider the add-on life span of any children or grandchildren after they inherit what is left over, which may be significant.

I more often prefer buying a mutual fund that is all stock or all bonds so I can easily identify my allocations and not be caught off guard later when long life spans occur, or conversely, markets crash.

Exchange Traded Funds aka ETFs - We're going to keep this real simple. When you think of ETFs, think of mutual funds. They are buckets of securities and can contain a variety of sectors just like other funds.

However, unlike mutual funds, ETFs *trade* more like individual stocks. For instance, if you put an order in at 10 o'clock in the morning to sell a mutual fund, the fund really won't price your order until the end of the day at market close. On the other hand, since ETFs trade like stocks, the trader's sell order will be recognized at the 10 o'clock current price, not a 4 pm closing price. If the market is sinking fast during the day, you can guess which one active traders prefer.

When ETFs were the new kids on the block several years ago, most were just index buckets and not actively managed for performance. Along with this came very low fees that investors loved. Most are still like this, but as they've grown in popularity, many new ETFs have a more managed profile to them. Make sure you know which type you're purchasing and its related fee.

One final thing about exchange traded funds. Unlike virtually all other types of mutual funds, many ETFs do not make it as simple to reinvest dividends automatically. I love reinvesting dividends and you should, too. For long term portfolios, that's where the compound growth can really kick in.

REITS or Real Estate Investment Trusts - Our financial world is such a beautiful place that, in addition to owning a piece of Apple Corporation or lending money to General Motors, we can also buy shares of ownership in companies that specialize in owning and managing real estate entities. We can choose REITS from a wide range of sectors, from companies that run shopping malls, or manage nursing homes, or enterprises that run fancy hotel properties.

What's even more interesting is that tax and investment rules require that such companies structured as REITs regularly distribute much of its income out to their shareholders. The result: Common stocks of REITs are usually very good dividend payers, becoming favorites of investors looking for good income combined with the potential for value appreciation.

As with stocks and funds, not all REITs are of the same quality, so shop carefully. One of the gotchas I see from time to time are REITs sold in various forms of legal partnerships structures; such entities come with liquidation restrictions, so if you want to sell them you cannot. That's no good for amateurs like us.

With tricky quality and liquidation issues, REITs are good candidates to buy in a fund, including a passive index, similar to the approach taken with preferred stock. Simply buy a fund bucket of REITS, do not panic with short term market fluctuations, and enjoy good income in the meantime.

Mutual Fund Naming Conventions—Deciphering the Code - Most funds have keywords or identifiers in their title to tell you what type of securities they're investing in. By knowing these descriptors, you can easily survey what the fund is attempting to do. This is very useful in managing a 401(k) account. Often the employee gets a menu or list of several funds from which to choose, then must choose percentage allocations among the funds. This process is much easier when you know the general lingo describing funds. Here are a few key terms:

Large cap - This is a fund of large companies—literally large capitalization companies. Similar to the S&P, but probably higher management fees than an S&P fund managed by a company like Fidelity or Vanguard.

Mid or small cap - Can you guess?

Growth - A fund with stocks of companies that may be younger and on a growth trajectory with their sales and revenue—but not necessarily its profits. These sound like a no-brainer to buy, but these funds may impose higher fees if managers of the fund are picking and choosing based on analysis, as opposed to a fund that is based on some existing index or list. Growth funds also tend to be more volatile.

Value - Stocks in these funds may be more mature and judged by the fund manager to be currently out of favor with stock buyers. The hope is that, in time, the good performance of the company will shine through and the stock price will pop higher. During the recent market boom and virus crisis, value stocks have not done nearly as well as growth funds. That could change as we move through highs and lows in the economy.

Index fund - A fund based on a given list of securities, either as a general group, such as the S&P 500 fund, or more specific sector, such as a collection of European stocks—or bonds. That's right, index funds can also be a group of bonds, for instance, a bucket of U.S. government bonds or high-grade corporate bonds. Index funds usually have very low management fees, and though simply based on a list of securities in a sector, they usually outperform comparable funds in which a manager attempts to select the best available.

International - Most funds described as international comprise stocks unless the title includes the term bonds. Funds that describe themselves as international funds can be vague because most large companies, even those originating from the United States, are international in nature. I usually don't like international funds because they include too much of what I don't know about and also because they're going to include countries that have much lower growth than companies based in the US.

High yield - If you see this term included in the name of a fund, it means that it is a bond fund and a high-risk bond fund at that. The bucket of bonds contains low grade companies and the securities are more commonly known as junk bonds. I usually avoid such funds, even though their income ratio is reportedly higher than other bond funds. Historically, the risk of principal loss outweighs the higher income rates.

Income Fund - Most funds that have the term *income fund* in the title means that they are bond funds. Bond funds, like bonds themselves, emphasize income and not appreciation in value. They are often good hedges against volatility in the stock markets. In the long term, however, as a category, they have not out-performed stocks.

Options Trading - If you want the headline for this term so you can skip it and go straight to the next chapter, here it is: Don't do it!

For those of you who are determined to swim with the sharks, here is a brief explanation. Like those options sometimes executed with real estate transactions, a stock option is a contract for which you pay a fee to buy or sell, usually a stock, at a later date, for an agreed upon price. As an illustrative analogy, in real estate, a potential buyer could pay the seller of a house a fee of $2,000 for the right to buy that house for, say, $250,000 within the next 12 months. The buyer's motive is to lock in a price and to be sure the house is still available if he wants to buy it. The seller is willing to do this because he is happy to lock in a selling price for a given time. And here is the fun part: If the buyer changes his mind about buying the house, let's say because he discovers a prior owner murdered his mother-in-law there, he simply walks away from the deal, not having to buy the house—that is, he does not *exercise* his option. And the owner keeps the $2,000 fee for his troubles of willing to hold the property available for a price of $250,000.

The principle with stock options is the same, but without the dead mother-in-law. A person buys an option (pays a fee) for the right to buy a stock at a given price by a given future date, say $100 per share. In the case of our stock buyer, however, he may not really care about owning the stock. He just cares that the stock price will climb enough to cover the price of his option fee plus additional profit. The winnings could be significant. If he pays $2 for the option fee for the right to buy the stock at $100, and the $100 stock climbs, say, to $103, he's just made a whopping 50% profit—he risked $2 and made $3 because the seller earlier agreed to sell the shares for $100 no matter what the stock price rose (or sank) to. Look at a normal stockholder who simply bought the stock for $100 and sold it at the $103 price. Her gain was only 3%.

Now the bad news: If the stock price in our example remained at $100, or rose to even $102, there is no reason for our option buyer to exercise, that is, carry through with, the option because the price did not cover his fee cost. In this case his loss is the entire option fee paid. In other words, his loss is 100%.

By the way, option traders can also pay a fee to bet that the price of the stock will go down; they profit by contracting to *sell* at a higher agreed price after they acquire the stock later at the lower price. Versions of this transaction are called *selling short* or *doing puts.*

The earlier example described above, that is, paying a fee for the right to *buy* a stock, is usually described as a *call* option, the opposite of a *put* option.

I must also tell you who typical option traders are, because the pattern is uncanny. It is always a man, in his forties or fifties, smarter than average with a level of previous success in business or in a profession, and with an ego higher than average. In the end, however, option trading performance is almost always under par. Think Las Vegas gaming.

Three Critical Takeaways from Chapter

1. You are not alone in your confusion about investing jargon.
2. There are thousands of many different type funds.
3. If you don't understand an investment concept, even after you investigate it, avoid it.

Chapter 5

IRAs and 401(k)s: How Many Different Types Can You Name?

Three Great Myths

1. An IRA is a *type* of investment, like a bank CD.
2. One IRA strategy fits everyone because, let's face it, the IRS has only one set of rules.
3. Roth IRAs are best because you don't pay tax when you eventually take the money out.

For this chapter I could make a list of 20 great myths. That's probably because we have so many confusing rules and regulations surrounding individual retirement accounts. For starters, here is a list of the different types of IRAs, and I have probably missed a few along the way.

1. Traditional IRA
2. Roth IRA
3. Backdoor Roth IRA
4. Non-deductible IRA
5. Beneficiary IRA
6. Estate IRA
7. SIMPLE IRA
8. SEP IRA
9. Rollover IRA

Have no fear. Because this is not a textbook, we will not review each one of these, nor will there be a chapter test. Indeed, the SIMPLE and SEP IRAs listed are primarily used for business owners and their employees. They are anything but simple, however. And for this basic manual, there is no way I am even going to try to explain a backdoor Roth IRA. That's what Google Search is for.

Soap Box Commentary: Our politicians deserve all the blame for the complexity of IRAs. No other country has such a convoluted system. A few administrations ago, in Washington D.C., there was a discussion to simplify retirement accounts to have one uniform savings bucket so that everybody knew how to put money in and how to take it out. Unfortunately, these discussions went nowhere. Instead, it seems that with each new tax law change we have new rules and new confusion. Politicians and their staffers may think they're very intelligent, but they are unable to design a simple retirement savings vehicle. Obviously, they'll never figure out how to balance the national budget.

First and most important to know, an IRA is not a type of investment but a type of *account* more closely akin to when we describe a joint account or a trust account. When an account is classified as an IRA, it implies legal rules for how people can put money into the IRA account, take withdrawals, and the resulting tax treatment one receives for various transactions affecting the account.

To the surprise of many, an IRA account is not just for bank CDs. Instead, view it as a bucket that can hold a wide array of securities and investments, including stocks, bonds, mutual funds, money markets, and of course the old standby, bank CDs. The IRA bucket can even hold annuity accounts, which we will discuss in chapter 8.

Given the various types of assets available to be owned in an IRA bucket there are also a variety of financial institutions that act as custodians (bucket-holders) for IRAs, including banks, mutual fund companies, stockbrokers, and insurance companies.

Are you wondering whether you can own real estate and private small company stock in an IRA account? Well, you can, but it's not so easy and attempting such transactions comes with pitfalls if you don't know what you're doing. It's also more expensive to administer. In industry lingo, they're called self-directed IRAs. I usually do not recommend this strategy.

A Traditional IRA - Your father's IRA, or, what we'll just call a regular IRA. You probably are familiar with this one. If working or self-employed with an annual net profit, you can contribute into an IRA account and get a tax deduction for it on your tax return. During the ensuing years, all growth and income generated in the IRA escapes annual taxation. Then you withdraw the money later, we hope much later, when retired and in a lower tax bracket. The withdrawals show up as income on your tax return. The 2020 limit for contributions is $6,000 if you're less than 50 years of age and $7,000 if you're older.

There is enough confusion to warrant repeating that this contribution into an IRA account does not have to sit in a bank CD where it may only get one percent or less per year. Research mutual fund and brokerage accounts or consult with a financial advisor to get the most out of this long-term investment.

The big gotcha with a traditional IRA for many people is that you may not be able to contribute if you make too much money and already participate in a pension at work. Your ability to contribute starts to phase out at $60,000 per year if you're single, and $120,000 if married.

A relatively new feature of traditional IRAs is that, if your legal spouse works, and you don't, you may contribute to your own IRA. This allowed deduction starts to phase out after the couple's income exceeds $196,000 (for 2020).

401(k) Plans in a Nutshell

A 401(k) is a type of pension plan administered by employers and named after the IRS code section that allows such plans. I mention these long-term savings vehicles throughout this handbook because of four primary advantages.

1. Forced Savings - By having payroll deductions made directly from work earnings, you never get the money in your hands, so you won't miss it as much. Refer to Chapter two for tips about how to save more money.
2. Tax Deductible - The amounts you have withheld to go into the 401(k) are excluded for calculating taxable income. The idea is the same as with traditional IRAs. Save taxes now while in a high tax bracket, then withdraw the money years from now in retirement when you probably will be in a lower bracket.
3. Free Pay Raise - Most employers match your contributions up to a defined level of earnings usually around 3%. Thus, if you deduct 3% of pay into a 401(k), they will throw in another 3%. This is free money! Now you have 6% going into long-term savings. Nice.
4. Good Investment Choices - Many 401(k) plans have come a long way in recent years in offering attractive investment choices to employees, usually a menu of various mutual funds. Tip: Choose the funds that have lowest fees and make sure your choices include stock funds (like an S&P 500 fund) that make up at least 60% of your allocations. (See Chapter 4 for a description of different types of funds.) A typical allocation structure may be something like 60% S&P 500 stock fund and 40% corporate bond fund. Now you're cooking, and doing much better than a bank CD or savings account.

For the advantages listed above, don't be afraid to use this convenient vehicle as your first and most important retirement tool.

Some companies offer Roth 401(k) options, but for most of us it is not advisable. Save the taxes now and contribute more with the taxes you can save.

Don't forget that you can transfer your 401(k) account from one employer plan to another when you change jobs. Upon job termination, you may also roll your 401(k) into an IRA at the bank or broker of your choice without tax consequence, which may allow you even more investment choices. Finally, you may borrow from your 401(k) account, but I strongly discourage using your pension savings to purchase a new car. Don't do it!

Contributing to an IRA plan, of course, is an important savings tool, but I suggest you work on maxing out your employment 401(k) contributions first as a priority. And, if your high income and 401(k) at work prevent your being permitted to deduct personal IRA contributions, an employee pension plan such as a 401(k), may be the only retirement savings option to receive tax benefits.

Traditional IRA & 401(k) Withdrawal Strategies

A gotcha with traditional IRAs and 401(k) accounts is that if you make withdrawals before age 59½ you may be penalized. You see, the IRS really wants you to keep these funds stowed away until it's time to go fishing. The tax penalty is 10%. But when you add it to your other income taxes, the overall rate for drawing out IRA money early could easily total 35%. Ouch! That's a big toll for withdrawing money to buy that new Mercedes. And what's worse is that this 35% handed over to Uncle Sam is no longer in your account to take advantage of compound growth. Using historical stock market growth rates, that means the money you kept *inside* the account will double in about eight years—and then double again in another eight years.

Get the message: After you sacrifice to contribute money to an IRA—or 401(k)—don't be punished again with taxes and penalties by withdrawing it early.

Are there exceptions to getting penalized? Yes. Here is a summarized list of excuses for traditional IRA's and 401(k)s you can use to avoid the 10% penalty—but you'll still be stuck with the income tax.

1. Withdraw funds after age 59½
2. Disability
3. Distribution as a result of a divorce settlement under a Qualified Domestic Relations Order (QDRO). Be sure a CPA guides you through this one.
4. Qualified higher education expenses (Early 401(k) distributions are not included in this exception).
5. A series of equal annual payments for retiring early. This exception comes with minefields. Get help from your CPA with this one, too.
6. Qualified first-time homebuyers can exempt penalty on withdrawals up to $10,000.
7. Withdrawals for unreimbursed paid medical expenses that exceed 10% of adjusted gross income.
8. You refund the IRA or 401(k) withdrawal within 60 days. In this case, the withdrawal also avoids income tax, but this refund exception is only permitted once during the calendar year.
9. Death. This is an excuse we hope we never need to use.
10. Eventually, politicians and the IRS want you to pay at least some tax on these funds you've been putting away for retirement and for which you've been receiving nice tax deductions. They've decided that in the calendar year you reach age 72, you must start to take some withdrawals, potentially triggering income tax liability. Required minimum distributions are often called RMD's in the lingo of the business.

Clients often suggest to me the idea of taking IRA distributions before age 72 on the theory that if there is less money in the IRA account when they hit the required age, the required distributions and resulting tax will be much less. For the vast majority of us, this early withdrawal theory is incorrect. In general, the longer you can leave your money inside the IRA to grow tax deferred, the better.

And what surprises many people is that when you reach age 72, the amount required to withdraw is very small, about 4% annually. This 4% amount increases gradually as you age, but not enough to require accelerated early withdrawals.

A reason you might want to withdraw IRA money sooner rather than later is if you find yourself in a zero or very low tax bracket, meaning that if you take the money out, you'll pay very little tax on the distribution. This is the ultimate win-win for the taxpayer because they received a nice tax deduction when they put the money into the IRA initially, but paid little or no tax when they take it out later.

Another reason you might want to withdraw IRA money sooner rather than later is if you know that, in addition to your being in a low tax bracket, your heirs, who are expected to receive the money after you're gone—are in a much higher tax bracket than you. Remember, if your wealthy daughter who is a doctor inherits your IRA, when she withdraws it for her own use, it will be taxed at a higher rate than you might incur.

Of course, a final reason to withdraw IRA funds sooner rather than later, especially if you can avoid early withdrawal penalties, is to simply enjoy your money. We all worry that we are going to run out of money or that will need a significant sum of it for medical care, but there are also many of us who can afford to enjoy life more than we do, but get into the rut of sacrificing for the future. Through all my years of observing hundreds of clients, I've seen very few who have accumulated significant savings then spent so much of it in retirement that they were forced to move into their children's basement.

Roth IRA

Named after the late Senator William Roth, the Roth IRA works in the opposite direction of the traditional IRA. With the *traditional* IRA, we get the deduction when we make the contribution and then we pay tax later when we make the withdrawal. With the *Roth*, however, we get no deduction when we make the contribution, but we pay no tax when we make later withdrawals.

Of course, there are tricky rules within the Roth that one can never remember. When we withdraw only up to the accumulated amount we put in, it is never taxable. If we have dipped into any of the accumulated earnings *over* what we contributed, then this part withdrawn is taxable and subject to the 10% penalty **if** the account has not been in existence for more than five years <u>and</u> you're under 59½ years old. This crazy rule therefore requires us to track and segregate our contributions (which come out completely tax free) from the ensuing growth portion of the account (which may be subject to tax and penalty if withdrawn too early). Moral of the story: Avoid withdrawals until you're at least age 59½.

And note: You can still avoid the 10% penalty on the accumulated earnings if you meet the same exceptions of the traditional IRA (see above), such as taking withdrawals to buy that first home or condo.

One of the major benefits of a Roth IRA is that not only can the account owner withdraw money tax free from their account, there are never any required distributions, even after age 72, unlike the traditional IRA. What's even better, an heir who receives Roth money from a deceased owner pays no tax when they inherit or withdraw the money. Very sweet!

Choosing a Roth or Traditional Deductible IRA

So, what's better, a traditional or Roth IRA, and if a Roth is so good, should I, and can I, convert my traditional IRA to a Roth?

If you can live without the instant gratification that a traditional IRA brings with it, do a Roth.

Let's face it, with the features of tax-free growth and tax free withdrawal that a Roth IRA provides, you really only want to do a traditional IRA if you can save a decent amount of taxes when you make the contribution. And also, let's realize that, statistically, about

50% of the working age population pays zero income tax and another 35% have a top tax rate of only 12%. The 12% tax rate is where most middle-class people find themselves. As you can see, for most of us, we don't save much income tax by contributing to a traditional deductible IRA.

Many financial experts point out that, if I make a $3,000 contribution to my traditional IRA, I save $360 in taxes. That's not much, but in theory, they assert, if I take the $360 I save and invest it, over time, that $360 saved can multiply several times. The problem with this theory is that most people don't put aside the $360 into an investment; they spend it. In this context, traditional IRAs quickly lose their advantage.

After the 12% tax bracket, the next tax bracket is 22%. This bracket includes single people that make more than about $40,000 per year and married people that make more than $80,000. These figures are approximations and come with exceptions to the rule, but I want to give you an idea for ranges and scopes. At this level of income and tax, I could be more easily persuaded that a traditional IRA is wise. The tax savings are nicer and saving even a piece of that for the future makes a traditional IRA a good deal here.

Several people counter this argument with the idea that when a person retires, they are probably going to be in the same tax bracket as their earlier working period. This may be true for some, but it is only valid if the taxpayer does not take advantage of reduced taxes by saving more, which I already argued that low income people normally can't do. In essence, most people are doing traditional IRAs so that they can save taxes this year in order to spend more money this year, then, hope to be in a lower tax bracket when withdrawing the money later in retirement.

For the immediate gratification of tax deductions that come with traditional IRAs, I believe there will always be an attraction for this savings vehicle. I witness this pleasant reaction when I'm sitting across the table for a tax return client and I tell them that by contributing $5000 to a traditional IRA, they can save $600 in federal income taxes and a few dollars more with state income taxes. In their mind, they've already spent the money before I can finish the sentence.

So, having outlined the statistic that most people pay very little if any taxes, and that most people don't invest what they save on tax deductions, it probably makes sense that, for most of us, a Roth IRA, in which we do not get an immediate tax deduction, is better, or at least no worse, than a traditional IRA in the long run.

Roths: Too Good to be True?

The important benefits of the Roth IRA: Tax free growth, no required withdrawals, and tax-free inheritance by heirs. Does all this sound too good to be true? Congress may eventually think so, too, especially as chronic out-of-control government spending continues. I advise clients that it is not inconceivable for the rules to change for Roths sometime in the future, especially for upper income taxpayers. Congress could tweak the rules, for instance, to disallow tax free distributions if the taxpayer's income exceeds $100,000. Or the rules could say that only the first $50,000 of a Roth account is inherited tax free.

You say that couldn't happen? In the past, other tax benefits have been reduced or eliminated in the name of budget balancing or, even more ironically, fairness. Alimony payments are now deductible for some but not others. Social Security income used to be tax-free for everyone—now it's not. Just a few years ago, monthly Medicare payments for retirees were equal for everyone. You guessed it: Now they're not.

Three Critical Takeaways from Chapter

1. You can invest an IRA in all kinds of savings vehicles, including stocks and bonds and mutual funds, not just bank accounts.
2. Roth IRAs are better than traditional IRAs for most of us, but we're all different. Check with a tax or financial advisor pro if in doubt.
3. IRA rules may—no, will—change. Stay alert for them.

Chapter 6

Life Insurance, or, *Actually*, Death Insurance

Three Great Myths

1. Life insurance has to be expensive.
2. Life insurance is a good savings vehicle.
3. You just need a couple hundred-thousand-dollar death benefit.

As with other areas of our financial lives, the jargon with this subject can be daunting. Let's review a few key terms without trying to sound like insurance policy fine print.

Insurance contract - When you buy an insurance policy, you are essentially signing a contract. You promise to do certain things and the insurance company promises to do certain things. One of the things you promise to do is not to lie on your application (about your age, health, etc.). Another thing you promise to do is to pay policy premiums to keep your policy alive. In exchange for these promises, the insurance company promises to pay money, usually at the time of death and, usually, when it's you who have died. This payment is called the death benefit. If the insurance company does not fulfill its terms of the contract, you or your heirs can sue them.

Policy owner - Usually the policy owner is the person who pays the premiums to keep the insurance policy active. In most cases it is also the person whose life is being insured. The policy owner is also the person who may communicate with the insurance company and who can possibly change original terms of the contract, if indeed the original contract allows anything to be changed.

Policy Insured Person - This is the person who has to die for the insurance company to pay out. Often it is the policy owner who has initiated the policy and has paid its premiums, but it doesn't have to be. Often, a company or spouse will pay premiums as the policy owner for the life of someone else.

Premium payment amount - The premium is the amount the owner of the policy pays to keep the life insurance contract active so that the insurance company pays out an amount upon the death of the insured. Premiums may be paid monthly, annually, or even all in one shot. If premiums are paid just once, the insurance is called a single premium policy.

Death benefit amount - This is the amount the insurance company promises to pay when the insured person dies. Perhaps beside the premium amount, it is the most important term of the insurance contract. Yes, in most cases the insured has to die to get the benefit. There are a few policies that an owner can have whereby the policy promises to pay before death if there are qualified nursing home costs that the insured incurs. But these are special policies. See chapter 18 for more discussion on insuring long-term care costs.

Beneficiary - Actually, if you are the beneficiary of an insurance policy, *this* is probably the most important part of a life insurance contract. The owner of the policy has designated you or someone else to receive the money when the insured dies. Upon the death of an insured, the beneficiary notifies the insurance company to start the process of paying out the death benefit. This process is called the claim process. Before the death of the insured, however, the beneficiary is not permitted to receive any information from the insurance company, including confirmation that he or she is indeed the beneficiary.

Whole life insurance policy - For this type of policy, your premiums go partly to pay for life insurance and partly toward an investment component, equivalent to a savings account. The longer you pay premiums, the higher the cash value is of the savings available for the policy owner to withdraw or borrow from, even before death. As such, on paper, this policy sounds great: a life insurance death benefit if you die, or if you want, have some of the money available *before* you die from the investment portion.

Unfortunately, the problem with whole life policies is that your premiums don't go very far, either for buying lots of death benefit or for accumulating cash value. For this reason, whole life policies are usually not seen as the best choice, despite what your cousin, who just got a job as an agent, tells you. What he also may not tell you is that whole life policies pay the biggest commission to salespeople.

Term life insurance policy - In contrast to a whole life insurance policy, term life policies can provide lots of death benefit at very little cost. However, there is no investment cash value that builds up over the time you have a term life policy. In essence, if you don't pay the annual premium, your policy gets canceled and you walk away or die with nothing. As bad as this sounds, most financial advisors recommend a term policy. It is not unusual for a term policy to provide 10 times as much death benefit as a whole life policy for the same cost.

Experts advocate that if you need life insurance and lots of it, load up on term life, and if you need to also add to your investments for savings, do that separately.

These policies are called term life because the premium cost is fixed for a term of years, usually 10 or 20. This is a really good deal because it means that after I have the policy, if I am the owner and person insured, I can count on fixed level premium costs over many years, even if I get sick or terminally ill.

Cash Surrender value - From what I have already described, you can probably figure this out. Surrender value is the amount of cash you have in the policy if you want to terminate before death. Term policies normally never have a cash surrender value. Whole life policies will have a cash surrender value, but it grows very slowly over many years. Most of the money you pay goes toward salesman commissions and very expensive insurance. For some policies, after an extended period of time, the cash surrender value may be big enough to produce income to pay part or all of the premiums. This sounds like a good deal at first, but you may be dead before you can reach this point.

Universal life insurance policy - Not as common these days, but every once in a while, a client has been approached by a salesman promoting these plans. Universal life is essentially a whole life policy, again, a product that offers a death benefit payout if the insured dies, plus a savings feature that builds up over the years. The benefits include the promise that, in addition to the death benefit, the savings portion can participate in stock market type investments whose performance will eventually pay the premiums. And this same accumulated investment balance will be there for you to withdraw before death as a tax-free loan after a number of years—sort of like a tax-free retirement income fund. Too often, high commissions, policyholder divorces, bankruptcies and detours in life contribute to the failure of universal life policies. I usually don't recommend them.

Real Life Strategies for Life Insurance

All right, John, you may say, I understand some of the terms, but I still don't know how much term insurance I should get. And do I even need it?

The first question can only be answered after we answer the second question and more specifically, for whom do we need insurance? In my view, if a person has no one depending on him or her for future financial support, or just refuses to create a benefit for others, there may be no need for life insurance. On the other hand, if you have a romantic partner, children, relatives, or even friends who would be financially hurt if you died, then you do need life insurance.

Ok, you say that you have a husband and child that would be financially stressed if you suddenly got hit by a bus. And that you believe they would need about, say, $50,000 per year to make up for what you could no longer bring to the family because you're, well, dead. How much insurance do you need to provide $50,000 per year for the next, say, 25 years?

There are a lot of theories and fancy formulas out there, but for the sake of this book on basics, use this simple rule of thumb: For whatever annual amount you think you need if someone dies, multiply that amount by 20. The result is how much death benefit you need when you buy life insurance.

So, back to your getting creamed by a bus. To replace an annual income of $50,000, you would have to purchase a life insurance death benefit of $1 million. (50,000 x 20. = $1 million). And that does not include an extra amount if you want to pay off the house, too, after the funeral.

Importantly, when heirs collect the million dollars from the insurance company, remember that this payoff is to be invested as the nest egg to provide income for the beneficiaries many years into the future. It is usually imprudent to spend large chunks of it the first year on cruises, cars, and Las Vegas vacations. It must be reasonably invested in an allocation of stocks and bonds so that it generates steady long-term investment returns. Let it be the goose that continues to lay annual golden eggs. If you kill the goose, you also lose the eggs.

Are you ready for some really good news after all this talk about bus crashes and dead geese? Term insurance these days is very inexpensive. For a healthy 30-year-old, a term policy that pays $1 million death benefit will cost about $500 per year. When you think about it, that's an amazing deal. Why is it so cheap? Simply because it takes many years for a 30-year-old to die, and also before we collect on it, many of us cancel our policy for a number of reasons and leave the insurance company off the hook. Policies lapse because we get divorced, our kids grow up and we believe we no longer need insurance, or the term runs out and we simply neglect to get a new policy.

When I buy term life insurance, I like to lock in my premium for a term of 10 or even 20 years.

Some of you may be reading this and continue to believe that life insurance is not necessary for your family if something happens to you. After all, you may be thinking, *my wife has a good job and she can support the family. And hey, after I'm gone, my partner will probably find a new partner for themselves, anyway, to make up for most of my lost income. Given these factors, I probably don't need insurance at all or if I get it, maybe I may need just enough to pay off the mortgage and a nice vacation for my surviving family.*

Wrong, wrong, wrong. The purpose of having death benefits paid to surviving loved ones is not for a luxury vacation. The real purpose for having life insurance can be summed up in one word: freedom. Receiving life insurance benefits after you're gone will allow your partner to have the freedom to live where they like, choose a job they enjoy, and even have a romantic relationship with someone they choose based on the freedom to dump that person if he or she turns out to be not a nice person, no matter how much money that new person may have. And think about this: If your surviving spouse has to settle for a mean jerk, that jerk will probably be mean to your kids, too.

Now that you know how inexpensive term life insurance is for the potential benefit received, another financial planning lightbulb should be turning on. Even if you don't have a spouse or someone that needs to replace lost income, a term policy is a wonderful way to instantly increase your assets upon your death if you want to magically leave a lot of money to someone you care about. This may be a good idea for a middle-aged person who has gone through life failing to save very much for loved ones but who wants to make up for it in a quick and easy way. Even at middle age, spending a few thousand a year for life insurance can create almost a million-dollar estate instantly upon your death. This strategy is great for people who are lousy savers but who still want to provide for heirs.

I almost forgot one of the best benefits of *receiving* life insurance proceeds as a beneficiary: They are tax free. That's right; if your favorite uncle named you as beneficiary of his life insurance policy, whatever you collect is not subject to any state or federal income tax. Yay!

When shopping for term life insurance, check with your local agent, such as the person who sells your auto insurance, but keep them honest by also comparing their quotes to those found through internet searches. You will be amazed at the bargains you find.

Using Insurance to Manage Risk

Life insurance is the ultimate risk management tool. The insured is reducing the drastic financial consequence of a premature death. In essence, however, all types of insurance are used to reduce the risks of life, from insurance for driving cars to insurance for confronting unexpected health costs.

The topic of risk management centers around the idea that through specific actions, the risk of losing assets and property is greatly reduced or even eliminated. It also means we reduce the stress that comes with worrying about loss of those assets. For most of us, having adequate insurance largely accomplishes this.

For many of my clients, I also recommend an extra insurance policy called umbrella insurance. This type of policy is a supplement used to pick-up where your other policies may stop. All of our home, property, and auto policies have maximums they will pay to someone coming after us in a lawsuit. The umbrella policy is there to help fund claims that exceed these policy maximums.

Is it common that our basic policies are not sufficient? No, in fact it's rare. But that's why umbrella insurance is relatively inexpensive. However, for those of you who have lots of assets, say in excess of $1 million, or own rental or other types of real estate that are vulnerable to litigation, I suggest you investigate this type of supplemental policy.

It is interesting to note that my experience over dozens of years with many clients has revealed that the most important ways to reduce the risk of loss of assets are not just through insurance policies but rather by avoiding major lifestyle actions. More than getting sued, the following life situations cause more loss of assets than lawsuits ever do.

1. Divorce - Or perhaps I should say, bad marriages. Divorce is especially a risky endeavor if one of the spouses makes considerably more than the other. In most states the law points toward splitting assets 50-50, particularly those that were accumulated during the marriage. I have seen the

successful doctor who married a high school boyfriend or girlfriend, and over the years, accumulated a good deal of wealth. Upon the divorce, the doctor can say goodbye to 50% of it.

2. Addiction - Addiction to drugs or alcohol is probably the riskiest lifestyle to choose. Most successful people who have this problem believe they can burn the candle at both ends, working and achieving while simultaneously leaving their addiction unchecked and untreated. The candle eventually burns out. At some point there is illness, poor work performance, or arrest.
3. Gambling - I probably could have included gambling in the *addictions* category but from my experience with friends and clients it probably deserves its own category. Gambling can be an all-consuming addiction with obvious financial repercussions. Check out gamblers anonymous if you need help.
4. Stupid investments - Ah, my favorite. Show me a successful professional, businessperson or professional athlete, and I will show you a brother-in-law or friend of theirs who has a great idea for the other person's money. I have seen a really smart person invest in a boat marina simply because the boat marina owner convinced him it would be a good idea. It wasn't. I have seen a successful physician invest in crazy oil and gas investments because his neighbor convinced him to do it. He shouldn't have. And of course, I've seen people who have a cousin or girlfriend or brother-in-law with the great idea to open a restaurant. It's guaranteed to make lots of money and be a fun place to hang out for the investor. Usually, however, there is no fun and the investor never talks to his cousin again.

Three Critical Takeaways from Chapter

1. Be careful when your cousin comes around trying to sell you whole life insurance policies, or a share ownership in his new bar.
2. Do not underestimate how much life insurance death benefit you may need—especially since the cost is so little.
3. Life insurance may be the best investment you ever make for this life—and the next one, too.

Chapter 7

Annuities: The Good, the Bad and the Totally Confusing

Three Great Myths

1. Annuities are good because the buyer pays no commission or fee.
2. Rates of return from annuities are comparable to stocks and bonds.
3. Annuities are the perfect solution for saving; annuities are a lousy solution for saving.

An Annuity is a Contract Between You and an Insurance Company

Annuities are sold by banks, brokers and insurance agents. However, you're actually doing business with an insurance company, which designs the contract and stands behind it. The other parties you deal with, usually the selling agents, are just that—agents.

Like any contract, each party receives promises from the other. I, as the buyer of the annuity, deposit money with the insurance company and usually promise to keep it with them for a period of time, often a long period of time. The insurance company, in return, promises me certain guarantees and features. The challenge for the consumer—even the trained financial analyst—is understanding all these features, because, in the annuity world, there are many different types of contracts with often confusing terms.

The idea with an annuity policy is that the customer deposits usually a significant sum with the insurance company for a promise of payments in the future. How and when payments to the customer start can be one of those confusing terms in the contract. Most of us buy an annuity with the intention that we will eventually receive steady, predictable, and long-term income streams, probably during our retirement. Obviously, the root word of annuity is annual, as in annual payments. While the insurance company has our money, we hope that our money grows so that we can get the most out of our later distributions.

The two most basic types of annuities are fixed and variable.

A fixed annuity is one in which the insurance company promises a fixed rate of return, almost like an interest rate, for some term. The fixed term rate may be for one year, or multi-year. Fixed annuities usually come with a guaranteed minimum interest rate, too. These days it runs around 2%.

On the other hand, a variable annuity is one in which the annual rate of return may vary all over the place because the contract is tied to some other factor, normally the stock market. Such policies may still have a guaranteed bottom, but usually nothing as predictable as a fixed annuity. Over the last few decades, variable policy terms and formulas have, in my mind, become incomprehensible to the average person—and even bewildering for some who are above-average. This could be a general formula of a variable annuity these days: Your annuity is tied to the stock market, but not exactly 100%, and if the market goes down one year, you will still have a higher value, but you must leave it in for some many years, and if you do, the future accumulated value is not the value you can cash in at, but only the value used to calculate annual payments you'll receive beginning at some later date.

I'm not kidding. The following complex wording is an excerpt from an actual annuity contract.

Your LIW income percentage is locked in for life. Payments are guaranteed as long as you live and will not decrease unless you take Excess Withdrawals from your contract or elect Income Withdrawals under the rider's Confinement Benefit or Terminal Illness provisions. Your Maximum Lifetime Income Withdrawal amount is based on a percentage of your rider's Benefit Base or the annuity's Accumulated Value, whichever is higher and is increased by the Early Lifetime Income Withdrawal Bonus Percentage, if applicable. The percentage depends on the income option you've elected, and whether you've chosen Single or Joint Life Withdrawals. The longer you delay taking income, the higher your withdrawal percentage.

Plain as day, right?

Let's contrast the confusing excerpt above with descriptions of two other examples of securities we've discussed:

- Description of a common stock: You pay $5,000 to purchase shares of Apple Corporation. Over time, if other investors in the stock market believe the company's value increases, the stock value increases; if other investors believe the company's value decreases, the stock price goes down. And you may sell your stock any time.
- Description of a corporate bond: You pay $10,000 in exchange for a contractual guarantee by the corporation to pay you 4% interest income per year until the bond matures, say, June 30, 2025. You can sell your bond at any time in the bond market before maturity and the price you receive may vary somewhat from your $10,000. But, if you hold your bond to maturity, you receive your $10,000 back in addition to the annual interest income you've received.

Of course, the description of common stock includes no guarantee, but I believe it is easier to comprehend than the aforementioned annuity clause. Perhaps that is why many successful investors shy away from annuities. They demand—and so should you—that they clearly understand where their money is going.

This is not to say that everyone should shy away from an annuity. Let's summarize the pluses and minuses.

Advantages of Annuities

1. Guarantees: There are often guarantees in the annuity contract, such as promised monthly payments, annual interest rates, or limits on value declines. These promises may be the most important feature for many owners, especially those with little knowledge of investment alternatives.
2. For terrible money managers: If you are lousy at managing money—perhaps you can't stop flying to Vegas for gambling

jaunts, or your kids are always begging to take your last dime—then putting a lump sum into an annuity might help preserve it. For instance, I know one lady in her forties whose husband died and left her with two spoiled teenagers and few assets except a $250,000 life insurance death benefit. By taking this lump sum and purchasing an annuity she was essentially able to lock her money up (refer to those nasty withdrawal penalties in Disadvantage #2 below). Later, when the kids cry poormouth, she can respond that her hands are tied because the money is stuck in the annuity. And she fixed her monthly distributions from the annuity as a regular income vehicle.

3. Monthly payments that never run out, if you choose: The owner of an annuity contract may elect various options for future distributions. Except for IRA annuities, from which you must begin distributions at age 72, most contracts allow you to delay commencement of distributions. When you eventually begin taking money from your account you can elect to take your money over different periods of time, such as five or 10 years. If you die in the meantime, your heirs receive the balance. However, you may also opt to take distributions that never run out during your lifetime. The good news is that you can always count on this monthly income no matter how long you live. The bad news: your heirs may not receive anything. I have seen this option work well for a single person who has no family to worry about, but just wants steady income for the rest of his life.
4. With some annuities you can elect to receive an extra death benefit beyond what your annuity value is. Expect to pay an additional cost for this rider benefit.

Disadvantages of Annuities

1. The soundness of an annuity is tied to the soundness of the insurance company selling the annuity. If the company is not financially sound enough to stand behind its guarantees, the policy owner will have problems. Fortunately, this is rare.
2. Your funds may not be very liquid for incidental withdrawals or changes of plans. Many annuities come with terms that penalize you if withdrawals are made before certain periods. These penalties decline over the term of the annuity. Some

annuities come with "bonus" rewards that many investors love taking the bait on. But be careful—the price you pay for such bonuses result in longer-term penalties on withdrawals and higher built-in fees. There is no free lunch. Note: Most contracts have an exception for withdrawal penalties that do not exceed 10% per year and for annual withdrawals required of IRAs.

3. The appreciation that may occur inside an annuity during the owner's lifetime will be taxed when distributed to the owner or to the owner's heirs. In contrast, owners of stocks and other assets have this appreciation forgiven when their heirs inherit such assets. This is called a *stepped-up basis* in tax lingo. For instance, if I buy stock in Amazon and during my lifetime that stock appreciates $25,000 in value, my heirs do not have to pay capital gains on the appreciation—if they inherit the stock after I'm dead. The same rule applies to appreciated real estate and even that Picasso original that you have hanging in the basement. It's a longstanding and well-loved tax loophole. On the other hand, if my annuity appreciates $25,000, I die, and my kids inherit this annuity, they must pay tax on the $25,000, and at regular income tax rates, not the lower capital gains rates.
4. The overhead structure of annuities eats into their rate of return, and normally much more than normal advisory fees. Insurance companies and the agents both have to get a piece of the pie. When people tell me that their annuity salesman told them there is no cost of commission to the customer, I explain that no one works for free—nor should they. Private agents and brokers may take a 7-10% commission. Even when a broker like Vanguard sells an annuity, they receive a commission from the issuing insurance company. I would rather know what my fees are than be told deceptively that there is no cost.
5. Annuities are usually not the best choice for retirees who are responsible managers of their money. The loss of stepped-up basis in assets, liquidity limitations, and inferior rates of long-term returns make such investments barely superior to bank CDs. But even bank CDs are insured by the federal government.

6. The surprise tax bill. We already talked about heirs getting hit with taxes upon inheriting annuities. I have also witnessed nightmarish experiences when the account owner withdraws a large chunk of old annuities to buy that second home or that long-desired sports car. All the accumulated gains built up inside the annuity suddenly become taxable. One person came into my office almost in tears. He started with a new stockbroker who convinced him to sell all of his annuities in order to buy securities the broker recommended. Unfortunately, the broker did not notice or did not care about the tax consequences. Cashing in the annuities created large additional income and drove the customer into a tax bracket he had never seen before. The tax bill exceeded $100,000. I could only give him a tissue to wipe his tears. Lesson to be learned: When the annuity salesman tells you annuity income is not taxed, don't believe him.

Annuities Can Hold IRAs, Too

The IRS gives us permission to put Individual Retirement Accounts (IRAs) into an annuity. This type of annuity is commonly called a *qualified* annuity. Some experts argue that putting an IRA into an annuity does not make sense because one of the theoretical advantages of an annuity—deferring taxes on the income generated by the annuity—is already available with the IRA. I compare it to wearing belts with suspenders simultaneously. Otherwise, all the advantages and disadvantages described above apply to IRA annuities as well.

Three Critical Takeaways from Chapter

1. One annuity contract differs from another. Read the fine print.
2. Experts agree that annuities are appropriate for only about 20% of investors.
3. Warren Buffett, the most successful investor in the history of the world, owns no annuities.

Chapter 8

Purchasing a Home—or Not

Three Great Myths

1. Owning a home is always a good investment.
2. You don't want to throw money away on rent.
3. A mortgage is ok because it's tax deductible.

These days, it is more difficult to buy a home than ever. Much of the blame rests with the great recession of 2008. Shortly before the recession it was quite easy to purchase a home. Banks would often require little down payment and even less paperwork to verify the new homeowner could actually afford the house he or she was purchasing. The result was that many people who purchased a home ended up way over their heads. When the bubble eventually popped, the inability to make monthly mortgage payments was the primary reason for the financial crisis.

These days it's very different. Banks are much tougher in their approval process. Lenders also require a larger down payment, often 20%, and they spend lots of effort verifying that the buyer can indeed afford the purchase. The result of these more stringent requirements means that a lot more people are renting. Renting has also become necessary as more young people, often saddled with college loans, move to expensive cities where high-priced real estate all but prevents home ownership.

But is renting really that bad? Most of us think it is. We've been raised to believe that a rental payment is money thrown away: We are not putting our money toward an asset to own outright later and perhaps cash in on. Many have believed home ownership is our best, and for some, only real investment.

But there are many disadvantages as well as advantages to home ownership. Keep an open mind as to which alternative is best for you. Everyone's situation is different and even though purchasing may be best for a friend, it may not be for you. Some of those plusses and minuses follow.

Advantages of Home Ownership

1. You'll eventually create an accumulated real estate investment. By paying that damn mortgage every month, over time, the less you owe means that more of the house value, including hoped for appreciation, can go into your pocket if you sell it.
2. As of this writing, mortgage interest rates are historically low. Low interest rates mean noticeably smaller monthly payments. For example, a 30-year $200,000 mortgage at 5% results in a monthly payment of $1,074. That same mortgage at 3% brings the payment down to $843, an annual savings of almost $2,800, enough for a decent vacation.
3. Perhaps better home maintenance. Studies have shown that people living in a house they own tend to care for the place better and are less rough on it. This translates into being able to live in a nicer place for you and your family.
4. Regular on-time payments to a home lender will increase your credit score, allowing you to obtain additional loans, such as those for autos, at lower cost.
5. You avoid those nasty rent increases every time your lease renews.
6. If there is enough equity in the house, that is, the amount you owe compared to its value is relatively small or zero, you may borrow against this equity. Some retirees use a technique called a reverse mortgage: Rather than making payments *to* a bank, the *bank* makes payments to the homeowner, utilizing the equity built-up in the home. A reverse mortgage cannot be done until the youngest

owner's age is at least 62. Costs and restrictions often greatly limit the advantage of a reverse mortgage, however, so be cautious.

7. You may gain an inner or social pride knowing that you have the perceived status of a homeowner.
8. Better neighborhoods. Often rental communities are not maintained as well as owner-occupied areas. Even if there may be less stress knowing the landlord will repair your air conditioner for free, you don't want new stress from living in a creepy, shabby location. (Fortunately, many new rental developments have gone the extra mile to create a beautiful living environment. They have stricter rules for their tenants and a higher monthly cost, but the result is usually a much nicer, safer experience.)

Disadvantages of Home Ownership

1. Most of your mortgage payment will go to interest, property taxes, and insurance with very little toward principal through most of the payment stream. Your money doesn't really start to put a dent in the principal owed until the latter part of the mortgage period. Most mortgages are 30-year mortgages with 35-year periods becoming more common. Statistically, however, houses are turned over on average about every 13 years as people move, get divorced, retire, or buy up. Over a 13-year period, little principal is paid, so your monthly outlay ends up being tantamount to a rent payment, anyway.
2. When you own a house, your "rent" cannot increase, but your property taxes and insurance do. If you think the three payment components of home ownership, that is, mortgage cost, taxes, and insurance, stay fixed, guess again.
3. The homeowner bears all cost of fix-up and maintenance. When you own a house that needs a new roof, guess who pays for it. On the other hand, if you rent and the roof leaks, you call the landlord. It's now his problem—and his cost. If a renter's air conditioner breaks on a Sunday night, he or she calls the landlord and complains to get it fixed. I

know, because as a rental landlord, I've received these calls. It's not fun.

4. Home ownership makes moving much less flexible. If you may need to move because of changing jobs or a family event, as a renter, you can usually terminate a lease pretty easily or simply not renew. Conversely, homeowners have to hang around and actually sell their house, which is often not easy or fast. In addition, the homeowner must make repairs and spruce up the place, which costs more money and effort. Accordingly, for a family moving to a new area, it may be smart to rent the first year in order to look around and get familiar with the various neighborhoods in the area.
5. For those lucky enough to be good savers, a traditional stock and bond portfolio historically appreciates more over time than do home values. Historical stock market increases average 10-12% per year. On the other hand, however, one study shows that, between 1968 and 2009, average home prices increased only 5.4%. And one of the reasons for this increase is that home sizes also increased. When size is factored in, the real rate is 3.7%. No matter how you look at it, home values grow less than securities.

I live in Florida and work a lot with retirees. I believe they are excellent candidates to rent. Maintenance worries are less. They can keep more of their savings invested. Moving to another location or downsizing becomes easier. There is generally less stress. What's even better, landlords love to rent to seniors. Retirees are stable and they do not destroy property. For these reasons, seniors can often garner very good rental deals.

If You do Buy, Remember These Tips

1. Don't count on favorable income tax deduction rules to save you lots of money. We've all grown up hearing that

mortgages are a good option because the interest is tax-deductible. It still is—technically. However, because new rules have raised the standard deduction to almost double what it was before, only about 15% of taxpayers even use the form where interest is deducted. On top of that, current mortgage interest rates are so low that many mortgage holders don't pay enough interest to get over or exceed the standard deduction thresholds.

Here's a simple example. A married couple purchases a house for $250,000, pays 20% down, and is left with a $200,000 mortgage balance. Their mortgage rate is 4%, so in the first few years their annual interest expense is about $8,000. Let's also assume they have property taxes of $4,000, state income tax of $5,000, and charity of $3,000. They have health insurance and are relatively healthy, so their out-of-pocket health expenses don't exceed the necessary 10% of their income.

When you add all of the itemized deductions, they total $20,000, not a small amount. But their standard deduction is $24,800 in 2020. Guess what: The itemized expenses do not exceed the standard deduction threshold, so they end up taking the standard deduction, the same tax benefit available to taxpayers who live cost-free in a tent. The homeowner has received absolutely no tax benefit from their mortgage interest.

2. Shop various lenders for the best deal. Too many of my clients simply go to the bank where their checking account is and settle for the terms offered there. I suggest you shop at least three lenders, including commercial banks, savings and loans organizations, and other lending institutions you find online. Compare not only interest rates but also closing costs. Typically, banks will make up for the low interest rate they offer by charging more closing costs. Remember, they are smarter than we are so you may need to seek a professional to compare numbers.
3. I love 15-year mortgage terms. If there is any way you can bear it, choose a 15-year mortgage over a 25 or 30 year, and

certainly a 35-year mortgage payoff period. To illustrate, if the homebuyer opts for a 30-year mortgage to pay off a $200,000 mortgage, the total interest paid over the term is $179,853. That's right; the interest paid is almost as much as the total amount owed. And that's assuming a historical low 4% fixed rate.

But look at this: If the buyer financed over only 15 years, the total interest paid would be $82,874, a savings of $96,979. And the cool part is that after 15 years, the monthly payment totally goes away! From that time forward, you have an extra $1,193 per month to enjoy—or save.

4. Don't get a 30-year term and try to make extra payments. Many borrowers enthusiastically tell me that they opted for a 30-year mortgage but promise themselves to make extra or higher payments during the term so that the mortgage payoff time is accelerated. I have not seen consistent success with this method. Often, the discipline is not enough to do this every month, and life gets in the way. I have also heard complaints that banks, and other lenders, do not properly credit the early payments. Just get a 15-year loan and dine a few more nights at home.
5. Try to avoid mortgages in retirement. I never like to see a client still burdened by a mortgage as they approach retirement. Indeed, I advise clients to have all mortgages paid off by age 62. You won't believe the reduced stress there is knowing that when you leave your job, a major expense in your life will not be there. Paying off by age 62 is not unreasonable for late starters if a 15-year mortgage is utilized. Thus, a person or couple age 47 can start and finish a 15-year mortgage payment plan and be done by age 62. Very nice.
6. If possible, don't even have a mortgage. In most cases, if a client can avoid a mortgage, I tell them to pay cash. Many investment advisors will overstate tax deductibility or advantages for setting funds aside for investments. Of course, the more the client mortgages, the more funds left

for the investment advisor. This is self-serving, and worse, often incorrect advice. As we've seen, tax savings from mortgage payments are little or zero. And, by using available funds to pay cash, you guarantee saving the interest charges of a mortgage. Most investments do not come with such a strong guarantee. The other nice thing about avoiding a mortgage is that closing costs are greatly reduced. No bank points are charged, no appraisal fees, and so many other expenses are eliminated. One caveat, however: Do not withdraw IRA or 401(k) funds to avoid a mortgage. The income tax toll makes this strategy prohibitively expensive.

7. For some, equity in a house may be their only asset. Let's face it, many are never able to save a dime throughout their adulthood. If structured payments to pay off a mortgage over several years build up equity, their home may represent the only real investment they own. Such equity may certainly help cushion a challenging retirement if they can live in the home "rent-free" or sell the home and move to a less expensive residence or rental. However, I usually don't see this as a proactive plan, but rather one where some people just end up. Unfortunately, many of these same homeowners borrow against their equity, or sell the home and squander the proceeds. For those of you who have equity in your home, cherish it.

Three Critical Takeaways from Chapter

1. Renting is often a reasonable alternative to home ownership.
2. Tax deductions for owning a house are mostly a thing of the past.
3. For those who are terrible savers, however, paying a mortgage may be the only way to accumulate an asset.

Chapter 9

To Marry or Not to Marry; That is the (Agonizing?) Question

Three Great Myths

1. Financial assets of spouses should always be combined.
2. It's easier for women these days to marry successfully because of their increased accomplishments and earning power.
3. The cause of fewer marriages today is due to strained finances.

Obviously, if you're already happily married, this chapter may be a pass for you, unless, of course, you have a child or other close person who is in a relationship contemplating the big step. And it is a big step. Perhaps more so now than ever. You may be surprised at the number of consultations I have regarding the decision to legally marry. Most of these discussions revolve around tax considerations, but they often evolve into issues of asset distribution, pension planning, and budgeting.

That the decision to marry is evolving rapidly is evidenced by the fact that a record few are doing it. Here are some fun facts about the changing times.

- In 1960, 60% of 29-year-olds were married, but that had dropped to only 20% by 2015.
- Today, a mere 16% of 18 to 29-year-olds are married.

- During the previous 100 years, the median age to marry was between 18 and 22. In 2016 it was 27 years (age 30 in cities).
- Half of births to mothers under age 30 are to unmarried women.
- More single women than single men are buying homes.
- Women born after 1990 drink as much alcohol as men their same age—a milestone since records have been kept.
- To sum it all up, over half of the US population is currently *not* married.

In some ways, there are as many reasons for people not getting married as there are single people. In general, I do not believe that finances or the tax code are the primary reasons. Social, career, and cultural factors probably play a more dominant role. For our purposes, we'll focus on financial and tax matters.

Financial Matters

With the increase of females moving into and up the professional ranks there is certainly less of a financial need for them to marry. Many women also realize that, once married, the accumulation of assets after that point becomes marital property which gets split in the case of a later divorce. If these are concerns you share, I make the following recommendations:

1. Get a prenuptial agreement. A prenup establishes an understanding between the spouses of how assets are to be split in case of divorce.
2. If you are already married, consider a post nuptial agreement. A postnup is often advisable if one of the spouses inherits a large sum during the marriage or begins a business partnership with others.
3. Even if you don't do some kind of nuptial agreement, consider managing income, expenses, and assets separately during the marriage. I know this sounds contrary to everything we have always heard, but a recent study shows that 60% of divorcing couples indicate that if they had to do it again, they would handle finances separate from their spouses.

4. Establish spending roles, especially if both spouses work. Example, I'll pay for all the restaurant meals, but you buy groceries at the market. I'll pay for vacations, but you pay the utilities.
5. Before tying the knot, if you still have the heebie-jeebies, consider taking the couple's survey below to gauge if each of you has similar expectations going into the relationship. The questions consider areas of careers, money management, family planning, and romance. I suggest you make a copy for your partner before you answer so that he or she can answer independent of you. If answers from each of you differ greatly, you will have problems. And, if you answer questions trying to anticipate how your significant other will answer, you are cheating—and dangerously fooling yourself.

PARTNER QUESTIONNAIRE: MY EXPECTATIONS OF THE RELATIONSHIP

Living Arrangement

1. In what location do I want to be living 10 years from now?

____

2. In five years, do I expect to be living in a condo, a small house, medium house, or large house? _______________

3. How many hours a week do I expect to work? _________

4. How many hours do I expect my partner to work? _________

5. How many hours per day do I expect to spend with my partner? _____

6. How many times do I like to eat dinner out each week? _____

7. My dream vacation would be:

____

8. I would enjoy having my partner's mother accompany us on vacation. Sure, or not really

9. It will not bother me if future children become identified with my partner's religion. True/False

10. It will not bother me if my partner belongs to a different political party than I. True/False

Finances

11. What do I expect to be earning annually in about ten years? ________

12. What do I expect my partner to be earning in about ten years? _________

13. What do I expect my monthly car payment to be five years from now? $________

14. How much money do I expect us to save away each year? $__________

15. I expect to have my own checking account separate from my partner's. True/False

16. I expect to reach an agreement with my partner before **I** make any purchase over $100.

True/False

17. I expect my partner to reach an agreement with **me** before making any purchase over $100. True/False

18. I expect to keep my pre-marital assets (real estate, car, etc.) titled separately. True/False

19. I expect to keep my pre-marital assets if we get divorced. True/False

20. I expect to have a prenuptial agreement if we get married. True/False

Love and Whoopi

21. How many children would I like? ________

22. What age do I want to be when we start having children?

____

23. Out of a 30-day month, it would be OK if my partner was work-travelling away ______ number of nights.

24. If I see my partner innocently flirting with an attractive person at a party, I (circle one) <u>will</u> or <u>will</u> <u>not</u> be very upset.

25. I expect that I will be hanging out with my friends away from my partner probably about ___ evenings per month.

26. I will be OK if my partner hangs out with his/her friends away from me ____ evenings per month.

27. My partner should probably expect me to get a little drunk or high approximately ______ times per month.

28. I will not have a problem if my partner gets a little drunk approximately _____ times per month.

29. I'm absolutely opposed to our using toys during sex. True/False

30. I'm absolutely opposed to our viewing porn during sex. True/False

31. I will be disappointed if my partner were to gain more than ______ pounds.

32. I will be disappointed if my partner spends more than ___ hours per week watching TV or gaming.

33. I will be disappointed if my partner does <u>not</u> spend at least ____ hours per week participating in exercise activities.

How did you both do? Remember, if you make this survey a discussion group project at a Starbucks before independent completion, you and your partner will find ways to come up with common answers. Take the survey separately and only afterward compare results.

Unlike taking a science test, you and your partner probably can't just easily say results were good if you answered 80% of the questions in common, which would be equivalent to a low B grade in school. Certain questions, and it may only take one or two, may be deal breakers for you. Yes, it's hard to take, but it's better to know sooner than later.

I know what you're thinking. All these suggestions and strategies seem very unromantic and awkward. However, we have seen that the alternative results in rather dismal national statistics: high marriage failure rates or no marriage at all.

An additional word about legal marriages versus just living together: If you think you avoid legal hassles by not tying the knot, you're wrong. When you split up it will be likely that you'll still fight over property, pets, and even children. A lawyer friend tells me that his divorce business may be down, but his child custody battle business is way up.

Tax Considerations

Should you just live together to save taxes? View this as a general rule of thumb: If your combined income is over $400,000, and income is around the same for each partner, it is downright more tax efficient *not* to marry. For the rest of us, it is generally pretty neutral, but you have to still crank the numbers with a professional who will consider your particular situation.

For instance, if a single parent has lower income, they may qualify for many of the low-income tax credits, including education and earned income credits. If that single person goes and marries a big hitter with lots of income, the credits are lost.

Another example is the federal limitation on state income and property taxes, now deductible only up to $10,000. That $10,000 limit is whether you are single or married. So conceivably, two single people can deduct $20,000.

Besides federal taxation, under our current laws, there are other incentives *not* to legally marry. It may be easier to acquire credit for that car loan or mortgage in one of the party's names if single. Otherwise, with a married couple, the person who has the lowest credit score will negatively impact the overall loan rate. Auto insurance is another area where the poor driving record of one spouse could affect the rates for both spouses. This is totally unfair, but that's the way it is.

Asset Protection Issues

In addition to tax and other financial reasons to marry or not, a couple should also consider the legal ramifications of owning assets separately, combined, or inside a legal marriage.

For this topic, you are going to be subject to the laws of your state, which vary across the country. For instance, in Florida, the state that I call home, marital assets jointly owned have an advantage against plaintiffs pursuing that property. If only one of the spouses is being pursued, the asset is normally protected. For instance, if I hit someone in a car accident and they pursue a piece of rental property that I own with my wife, the plaintiff probably can't get the property if my wife was not a party to the car accident.

It may be different in a different state. If a married couple does not have that protection, I would probably not want to have property owned jointly in a legal marriage if my spouse were an alcoholic and likely to be sued for dangerous driving incidents.

As you read through the strategies, it becomes easier to understand why fewer people are legally marrying. I am not sure which came first, however. Did rules favoring singles encourage people not to marry, or did all the single people influence how lawmakers adapted rules and regulations?

The same attorney friends I mentioned earlier claim they are also busy with settling joint property disputes for non-married couples who split. If you are not legally married, I strongly recommend separate ownership of assets.

The Promise Marriage

These days, how are couples avoiding divorce? By avoiding marriage.

One possible alternative to the marriage versus non-marriage issue is something I call the Promise Marriage. The following are excerpts from another book I've authored called *Unconditional Love Sucks: How an Old Myth Ruins Relationships.*

Some have called the Promise Marriage a spiritual marriage, but it is really much more. A promise marriage frequently consists of a public ceremony, like a wedding—perhaps with religious clergy, in which the couple makes a long-term commitment to each other before their friends, family, and children, if kids are already in the picture.

It is up to you and your partner whether to tell others that you decided not to stop by city hall for a license. As a result, nobody has to know, and, indeed, as we move into the future, more and more of us will care less and less about the state legally sanctioning the relationship.

Benefits of Rings Without the Contractual Slings

There are several reasons a Promise Marriage may be a good solution for many couples:

1. Children have more domestic and familial security knowing that their parents are in a committed, long-term marriage.
2. Income, assets, and debt may continue to be managed separately, which is what I advocate for all couples.

3. If you don't tell people it's a non-licensed marriage, they won't ask.
4. You both know that you cannot take anything for granted; you're with each other because you want to be, not because of a legal contract.
5. It eliminates the need for a prenuptial agreement. Only about 3% of marriages get a prenup, anyway.
6. You avoid various "marriage tax" penalties.

Also be aware of the following:

A. A prenuptial agreement may still be needed in common law marriage states in which rules in place determine how assets are to be allocated between partners in a break-up if there is no prior agreement or legal marriage. As a note, Florida is not a common law marriage state.
B. If one of the partners never works outside the home, and will have earned less income than his or her mate, this person's surviving Social Security benefits at retirement age may be less than if legally married. This is much less of an issue with both partners working.
C. Some states offer special asset protection benefits for legally married couples not available to other couples. I have seldom seen this come into play, however, and separate ownership of assets more than offsets the advantage that comes with a legal marriage.
D. Your pastor or rabbi may frown upon a promise marriage. This is a bit ironic since you would think their focus on personal spirituality and commitment overrides what civil lawmakers create. If this is a problem, perhaps find a new pastor.

Three Critical Takeaways from Chapter

1. There are probably more advantages for *not* being legally married under current laws.
2. Try to manage income and assets separately whether legally married or not.
3. Seek legal and tax advice! Situations are different for different couples, and that which is appropriate for your cousin may not be for you and your partner.

Chapter 10

Planning for College Costs—Yes, There is Good News

Four Great Myths

1. In 10 years, colleges will look a lot like today but with higher costs.
2. College loans will be available in the future as they are today.
3. College savings plans like 529 plans are tax deductible.
4. 529 plans are usually the best savings vehicle for college.

Before we even think about how we save for someone's future college costs, we need to review the college landscape—currently and for the future. For this task I need to put the hat on I wore as vice chairman of the board of trustees for a state college in Florida, as well as past chairman of its fundraising foundation. Much of this chapter is directed to parents, but is also a must read for students as well.

Currently, the conventional view of an undergraduate experience includes approximately four years (often more these days) of courses on a campus with classrooms, instructors, and if you live around the university, lots of beer parties. Add up the cost of tuition, books, campus fees, room and board, and of course, beer, and you have a massive investment, often more than that required for buying a home.

It's no wonder college debt is at record highs.

How We Arrived Here

The good intentions of politicians have created a nightmare for college affordability. Over the years, government has facilitated easier money for financing college in the form of loans and grants. This in turn has allowed colleges to raise tuition relatively painlessly knowing that such increases would be readily funded. The result: a long-term revolving cycle of more loans and rising costs.

Forty years ago, I was a low-income kid who dreamed of attending a private college. I took a shot, and by commuting, working two jobs, and getting a small grant and loan, I did it. However, now when I see what the current tuition is of my alma mater, it would scare me away from even applying to such a school that promises what seems to be a lifetime of debt.

According to Business Insider, between 1980, when I attended college, and 2014, average consumer prices climbed 120%, but tuition skyrocketed 260%, more than double the inflation rate. No wonder I'd be afraid to attend my chosen school.

Pretty much like the housing crash in 2008, everybody has a share in the blame for the escalation. Politicians made loan and grant programs too generous, universities have been creating country clubs for students, and students were not realistic in their budgeting. Perhaps more undergrads should have waited on a few more tables, too, in between classes.

Student population has been dropping in recent years, and universities, especially smaller private ones, have initiated capital improvement projects, like the country club ones cited earlier, to attract new students. One administrator of a well-known university told me, *It's one thing to get entering freshmen; it's another to retain them through graduation.* His college has created the gym of the future to attract students. On my tour it appeared that every student had their own treadmill—equipped with a smart television. The four-year cost at this center of higher learning—and aerobics: $280,000.

But here's the big news about the college of the future: It won't look anything like today's college. That is, unless you simply want a campus party-hardy experience. For the most part, the campus of tomorrow will be virtual. Students will be doing most of their course time and class work from a table at a Starbucks or on a bench in the park. Don't be dispirited by this future. I've seen courses on a computer that are entertaining, stimulating, and utilizing graphics that can easily out-do the classroom experience—and these courses are getting better every day. The creative ways to deliver learning information is endless, whether the topic is microbiology or Picasso. Think about it: For your art history course, you would probably prefer the best lecturer in the country along with highly interesting graphics, interactions, and illustrations over a tired professor in a dark class going through old slides while you try to keep awake. The former choice is the future of college education, the latter, the stubborn status quo.

I say stubborn because most colleges and faculty do not want to give up their empires. They see the future, too, and they are scared to death. As a result, many colleges are downplaying the future potential of course delivery alternatives *("How will we test students on material?")* while they simultaneously create online courses themselves as a gesture of keeping up with the trend. Unfortunately, if a professor is mediocre, the online course will likely be mediocre.

In short, in as little as 10 years from now students will have readily available to them many accredited courses and programs they can select that will be more attractive—and much less expensive—than those offered in large lecture halls conducted by graduate students. It's even probable that the primary function of colleges will be to counsel and provide career guidance rather than classrooms. Of course, the student will pay for such counseling service but probably not as a part of a tuition package. He or she can then choose inexpensive online courses from a universal catalogue that makes available the best of the best.

As a recent governor of Florida declared to me during a meeting with him, "College costs will come down in the future, but if the student wants to go somewhere to party, he or she will have to pay more for that."

It's amazing that many of these big university campuses offer more and more courses that are classified as online, but the school's tuition has not come down. Administrators claim continued overhead cost, but that excuse will fall short as competitors find a way to offer better and better online courses at lower and lower cost.

The result of this revolution in higher education will be dramatically reduced costs. Currently, the average annual tuition for community colleges is $3,500, for in-state universities about $10,000, and for private undergrad schools, approximately 35,000. On average, a typical full-time student takes 10 courses per year, which results in a charge of $3,500 per course. Contrast this fee structure to some accredited four-year online colleges able to charge less than $4,000 *per year*, or $400 per course, a reduction of almost 90%!

What could stop this avalanche of change? College administrators are putting pressure on regional and national accreditation bodies to slow approval of online courses and programs. But that may be difficult to do for long because these same administrators need *their* online courses accredited, too. In 2020, the impact of the Corona virus has amplified the opportunities for virtual learning.

Wow! This coming revolution in higher education is a lot to think about—especially when planning for costs and grants and loans. Here are some ramifications of the new financial landscape:

1. Lower tuition for coursework.
2. Extra fees for live, in-person classes.
3. Fewer people on campuses.
4. Smaller colleges close down or merge.
5. Less sense of loyalty/attachment to one school. Future students may not be such passionate Buckeyes or Gators due to diverse sources of coursework leading to degrees from multiple universities or colleges.
6. Reduced availability of state and federal grants and loans.

7. Broader range of available professionally-produced, creative, and compelling online courses—at a low cost to the student.
8. Mitigation of excessive annual inflation of higher education costs.
9. Encouragement for more students to reside with parents while completing their education, thus reducing costs further. Sorry, dad—or perhaps, grateful dad—depending on who pays the bills.

After all of this peering into the crystal ball of the college of tomorrow, I hope you are convinced and even optimistic that future college costs may not be the nightmare they are today. Unfortunately, tomorrow does not mean next week or even next month. This evolution will occur over several years. What this means to you is that if you or the student in question is about to attend college next year, many of these cost-reduction factors listed above will not be in place or even evident unless you scour the horizon for accredited online colleges.

On the other hand, if you were planning to finance college for a child currently under 10 years of age, I believe you have much to look forward to, and many opportunities to reduce the amount you must put away. As hard as it may be to believe in this age of outrageous college costs, I am convinced that a child under 10 years of age today will be able to receive a world-class college education for less than $20,000. Of course, this does not include room and board at a fancy party-campus university. In short, the younger the child, the less expensive their college costs may be.

Based on the type of school planned (community college, state university, private college, and don't forget accredited online school) and current age of the student, you should be able to calculate expected costs.

In planning expected costs, don't assume the receipt of grants, loans, or volleyball scholarships, which could lead you to underestimate cash needed as well as inaccurately predict the *type* of college a future student can attend. Underestimating cash requirements may also prevent you or your child from planning the necessity of working part time jobs while attending college.

Such misplanning of future expenses will leave the student in more debt after school. I hate college debt, and you should too. Target to have zero debt by graduation. If that's impossible, it should at least be no more than a small car loan. Students are not saddled with lots of loans because they have a poorly paying job after graduation. They're burdened because they did not plan properly for the cost before starting college.

Now that we've reviewed various college options and their cost ramifications, let's take a basic look at ways to save money for a future education.

529 Plans

A 529 savings plan is the common vernacular for an account that lets the saver put money into a bucket and as it earns interest or appreciates in value over time, the growth portion of the account will not be subject to income tax. Period. The number 529 comes from IRS code section 529 that allows tax-free growth on college savings if all rules are followed.

One of the big myths is that using a 529 for savings results in a tax deduction for contributions to the plan. Wrong. Instead of offering tax deductible contributions, these accounts offer tax-free *growth* so that when you withdraw the funds for college there is no income tax to pay on the interest, dividends, or appreciation. However, I am going to show you that there are alternatives to these plans that also offer tax-free growth without all the rules and limitations imposed by 529s.

Prepaid Tuition 529 Plans - First, let's talk about the type of 529 plan that lets you pre-pay tuition for college costs in the future. This sounds like a very good deal because you put money into the plan over several months (or perhaps one lump sum payment) before the student reaches college age. The earlier you start, the lower the monthly payments. The state in which you reside, and to which you make these payments, promises to cover the student's tuition costs at an in-state school or an eligible private institution. Based on the age of the child and the type of program you choose, the state gives you a fixed monthly payment amount and voilà, when your child starts school, tuition and fees are paid out of the plan. Again, there is no tax deduction for contributions, nor are the payments for tuition taxable income to the student or parent.

If this sounds like something in which you'd like to participate, don't get your hopes too high. There are only eight states that still offer the prepaid tuition guarantee. And by next year, this number may be even smaller.

The remaining states deserve a round of applause so I will list them:

Florida
Maryland
Michigan
Mississippi
Nevada
Pennsylvania
Texas
Washington

Other states offer prepaid tuition programs but do not include guarantees. That is, they let you make monthly payments into the program, but do not promise that these payments will cover all of the future tuition for your child. The obvious reason: they don't feel comfortable giving you, the parent, such a promise, because they know about the recent history of spiraling college costs and they expect it to continue.

If my predictions are true that college tuition will be coming down in the future, guaranteed prepaid tuition programs may not be a good deal, anyway. That is, the eight states that still offer such plans have built into the cost the historic inflation we've seen with higher education. If this inflation suddenly becomes deflation, the parents and students who have paid into this prepaid tuition program may be overpaying. Generally, if you pay into a state's prepaid tuition program, for optimum benefit, you are betting that the student is going to be attending one of their qualified schools or programs. This limitation will narrow your education options, especially in a future world that promises to offer many creative and cost-saving alternatives.

Bottom line: I do not recommend guaranteed prepaid tuition programs.

529 Savings Plans - The other type of 529 plan is typically called a 529 savings plan. This is one in which usually the student's parent or grandparent or some other benefactor makes contributions to a special savings account to be used later for college tuition and fees. More than half the people I talk to about this plan initially believe that contributions are tax deductible. They are not. Many also believe that such assets will not be included when applying for financial aid later. They are—usually. Currently, 529 accounts will not be included if owned by grandparents, but guess what, when withdrawals are made from grandma's account, such withdrawals are counted as student income, which could also reduce financial aid. They seem to get you one way or another.

The only good feature of a 529 savings plan is that accumulating growth and income in the account is never taxed—when withdrawn for qualified college or k-12 private school expenses.

Unfortunately, if you withdraw funds for other reasons, such as, the student decides to become a plumber or to use the funds for a new car, there is a 10% penalty—and lots of paperwork—on those annual earnings accumulated in the account. And, if you find inexpensive online courses and ultimately don't need all the funds, you still pay the 10% penalty unless you meet one of the exceptions (disability, scholarship, death, etc.), and unless the account can be transferred to another related student beneficiary.

Sound complicated? It is.

I do not recommend 529 savings plans unless all of these are true:

1. Your future college student is less than 5 years old. Such a youngster will still have another 13 years until starting

college. In the case of doing a 529 plan for K through 12, you should probably start soon after birth. Why? The more years you have to let the investment grow, the bigger the likelihood for extensive tax-free growth, and therefore more worth going through all the paperwork.

2. You're contributing many thousands of dollars to the plan, say at least $20,000. If just nickel-and-diming, the tax-free growth will probably not be significant, and therefore, also not worth the paperwork or compliance issues.
3. You don't believe me that the college landscape will change, and are convinced that your student is most likely to attend an expensive campus-like university setting.

Alternatives to 529 Plans

The context of the following alternatives to using 529 for a college savings revolves around the fact that, first, 529 plans create little tax savings for most people, second, their value is often included in financial aid forms, and three, the investor loses a large sense of control over these funds. I have not mentioned the higher fees that some 529 plans charge and their limited investment choices. Here are some savings *alternatives*:

<u>Roth IRA</u> - With this idea, typically the parent or grandparent of the student sets up a Roth IRA, not in the name of the future student, but in their own name. The benefits of this strategy include: IRA assets are not included assets in FAFSA (Free Application for Federal Student Aid) standard forms; you avoid 529 restrictions about using funds only for education; you can normally withdraw funds penalty-free for education expenses; and, if you don't need all the money for school, it's no big deal, the parent or grandparent can use as he or she wishes.

But a Roth IRA is not perfect. You still don't get tax deductible contributions and their annual limits, about $6,000 per year, are less than 529 plan limits. Even $6,000 per year, however, may be enough if you can start early and you are smart about university choices, especially given the evolution of the college of the future, as discussed above. Many advisors recommend you max out the Roth IRA, then put the balance in a 529 plan.

UGMA - The law allows us to set up accounts for minor children, putting the ownership in their name and Social Security number, but which the parent or grandparent controls. This type of account is called a Unified Gift to Minors Act account or UGMA. This choice should at least be considered because it gives us total flexibility with investment choices, it is low-cost, and there are no education expense requirements if we change our mind about the child attending college. Because the account is in the child's name, earnings will be taxed at the child's rate unless annual *investment income* generated in the account exceeds $2,200. Annual dividends and interest income exceeding $2,200 may be taxed at the child's parents' tax rate.

This is probably the most important point about all this planning for a student's future education costs: With the current tax rate structure, stock dividends and long-term capital gains are taxed at very low and even zero rates. So, the taxes we are trying to avoid with all these complicated 529 plans is not very much, anyway.

What is more, many growth stocks and similar funds pay little or no dividend in the first place, eliminating the need to worry about tax on income because there isn't any. In non 529 accounts, as stocks appreciate over the years, this annual appreciation is not subject to tax until the stock is sold. And capital gains tax rates for most of us is zero. For example, if you buy Apple stock in your five-year-old's UGMA account and it triples in value by the time that five-year-old reaches college-age, that appreciation is a capital gain. If it is sold in your child's account and is not subject to the kiddie tax, it will probably escape income taxes.

Many critics of the UGMA strategy declare that such assets will be included as student assets in the financial aid application process. True, but if they're not very significant in value the effect will be minimal. Critics also cite that once the child reaches the age of majority, which is 18 in most states, the child has full legal control of their money. Also true, but I have never, and I repeat never, seen a student or child upon their 18th birthday call up grandpa and tell them they're taking the money out to buy a new Porsche. Most kids don't even know the account exists and those that do, have no idea how it works.

Gift to poor relatives - Let's remember our goals as we save for college costs. We want to avoid taxes; we would like the funds unrestricted; we would love it if the assets could be excluded for calculating financial aid eligibility; and we would like to minimize management fees on the investments that we hope grow as much as possible over the years between birth and college. Believe it or not, we can pretty much accomplish all these objectives if we can do one thing: find a relative or very close friend that we can entirely trust who is in a low tax bracket. We then gift our contributions to this person who opens an account in their name and titles it as a transfer on death back to you or the student. In this way there are no use restrictions on the money, it will grow tax-free given the relative's low tax bracket, and if he or she dies in the meantime the money will transfer back.

But be careful. This cannot be a loan or some other restricted transfer. It must be an outright gift so that it does not amount to legal deception. And, because it is an outright gift, that poor uncle has every legal right to take the money and his new girlfriend on a trip to Hawaii. The understanding must be that it is no longer your money and that your trusted friend will gift back the money when it's time to pay Junior's tuition.

Do Nothing - The last alternative, which I don't think is entirely unreasonable, is to do no special savings account, no 529 plan, and no gift to your crazy poor uncle. The parents keep the money in a normal investment account as part of their own regular and retirement savings funds. In light of expected declining college costs and expected increase in retirement costs, *mom and dad* will probably need all the money they can gather for their own later years. Then, if the child *does* need funding for college, we can more easily determine which and how many assets to liquidate. In this way, parents don't have to worry about 10% penalties, mysterious 529 management fees, and making sure all the money saved for college is spent on college.

Hey, and if you're lucky, maybe your child will enter a military academy, or even better, become a plumber.

Three Critical Takeaways from Chapter

1. More affordable college costs are coming, and maybe sooner than you think.
2. If you end up borrowing more than $20,000 by the time of completion, you either could not afford the school in the first place, or the student had too few part-time jobs while attending.
3. A 529 plan may not be the best alternative to save for college.

Chapter 11

Vehicles: Driving a Good Bargain

Three Great Myths

1. Used cars are unreliable.
2. It is always better to pay cash for a car.
3. Purchasing a vehicle is less costly than leasing.

One of the financial chores most of us perform in the trenches of life is to acquire a new vehicle. Besides matters of personal taste, such as color and choice of sound system, financial issues usually boil down to three:

1. Do we buy new or used—excuse me—pre-owned?
2. Do we purchase or lease?
3. Do we pay cash or finance?

New or Used?

From a financial, dollars-and-cents perspective, this is probably the easiest question to answer, not only in this chapter but in the entire book. When you crunch the numbers, it is overwhelmingly obvious that one should never buy a brand-new car. It is even more the case now when the quality of cars has risen dramatically during the last several decades.

Typically, automobiles depreciate in value about 20% per year. This means that after three years they're worth about half their new showroom price. It also means that if you were the one later buying that three-year-old pre-owned car, you would save about half of the original purchase price.

If we estimate that an average new car costs $30,000, the new car purchase loses approximately $15,000 in three years. If I had bought the car used, it would still depreciate, but let's say that if it depreciated the same 50%, my depreciation cost (lost value) is only $7500, not $15,000. In short, over a three-year period, I've saved the difference between $15,000 and $7,500, or $7,500. This averages $2,500 per year.

An annual savings of $2,500 may not seem like much, but if you could invest this $2,500 per year over, say, 25 years at 5% (half of what the stock market historically averages), you would accumulate $125,000 in savings. Now that's impressive.

According to the National Automobile Dealers Association, the average person will own 13 cars in a lifetime—a tremendous amount of depreciated value if you constantly buy new.

Some car lovers are honest with me, declaring they just prefer new cars. They like the new car smell and enjoy boasting to friends they have the latest gadgetry. Others claim that purchasing a new car is necessary in order to be assured of reliability and low maintenance costs. That might have been true 25 years ago, but it probably isn't today. Newer preowned cars are built better, last longer, and require less maintenance. When I was younger, I had to tune my car—I actually did much of it myself—at least every year. This involved a list of tasks including changing spark plugs, distributor cap, and spark plug wires. These days, most cars don't even have spark plugs to change. Other maintenance chores like tire rotation and replacing air filters have to be done with any car, new or used.

Modern cars typically don't need tune up maintenance until they're close to having 100,000 miles. If you're buying a pre-owned car with fewer than 50,000 miles, you're probably saving lots of money and getting an excellent vehicle. Many factory warranties also go out to 100,000 miles and may transfer to the new owner. Some warranties, however, may reduce upon transfer, so research this before you purchase. Also, investigate prior accidents of a car you're considering using a resource such as Carfax.

If you are still concerned about maintenance and reliability, check out cars that are certified preowned or CPO. These are cars that are typically less than four years old, have fewer than 48,000 miles, and often come with an extended warranty by the dealer. I've owned CPO cars and they've performed well.

When people tell me that one advantage of purchasing a car new is the likelihood of receiving lower interest rates on financing, I would counter that the lower rates don't make up for the higher purchase price. In addition, borrower interest rates have been chronically low—and therefore, the difference is insignificant.

Lease or Buy?

In my view, the lease or buy issue is a little grayer than the new-or used debate. I traditionally advise that purchasing a vehicle is better in the long run because at the end of your monthly payments you have an asset—the car—owned outright.

The typical auto lease works this way: The dealer's finance manager and bank work out a monthly payment you owe, based on a negotiated vehicle price and calculated interest rate. Both factors must be disclosed to you, the consumer. Indeed, you should come to the dealership armed with researched price information. Check out Consumer Reports, Edmunds, or other vehicle valuation sources. Settle on the price before you disclose you would like to lease. Also make sure you know the implied interest rate the dealer is using for your deal.

Some other important factors that determine your monthly lease amount include agreed-upon miles allowed, maintenance extras added, and the down payment amount.

For leases, the average annual mileage allowance is 12,000 miles. If you exceed this annual amount over the typical term of the lease, three years, then the dealer charges you a penalty rate per mile, which could be very steep. If you drive a hundred miles to work every day, you probably don't want to lease.

The higher the down payment, the lower the monthly lease payment. One of the advantages of a lease is that you could probably get into a car for a smaller down payment than if you were purchasing. Another way to look at this is that you can probably be driving a more expensive car for a smaller down payment and with a smaller monthly payment.

The smaller monthly payment for a lease results because you're not paying for the full residual value of the car; you're really only paying for the depreciation of a car during the time of your lease period. On the other hand, monthly payments on a purchase include the cost of the depreciation plus the residual value left after payments are complete. An auto finance manager and dear friend put it this way: The car dealer will always take your money, but you should normally *own* appreciable assets and *lease* depreciable assets.

Accordingly, if you: 1) cannot or will not pay cash for a car; 2) you like to drive new cars with all the latest bells and whistles; 3) do not drive more than average miles, and 4) you want to reduce monthly payments, a lease may not be a bad idea.

Rapidly changing automotive technology may be another reason to lease. My wife currently owns an electric hybrid automobile. We don't know what the trade-in value will be and are a little concerned that enhanced battery technology on new cars will make the battery in her car somewhat obsolete. She wants her next car to be fully electric. For this new acquisition we may lease because, after three years, we don't have to worry about whether the vehicle she is driving has become obsolete. We simply turn the car into the dealer and walk across to the show room and test ride the latest razzle dazzle available.

That's my wife. She likes cars and she likes new ones. But I'm different. Give me a 10-year-old pick-up truck with a half decent radio and I'm happy. I love not having any payments and I would probably be the last person to lease. As you might imagine, I also need to understand exactly what I am paying for and how the numbers add up. Can *anyone* really decipher an auto leasing contract, except perhaps the dealer finance manager? I'm going to buy every time.

Leasing a pre-owned vehicle: Yes, many don't know this, but it is also possible to lease a used vehicle. Most of these are done through dealerships with so-called certified preowned vehicles. Call the dealer first to verify that it participates in such programs and don't forget: You still have to research fair price before you arrive on the lot to face a clever salesperson.

Some final notes about leasing that I hinted at earlier. Because your monthly payment is not only based on the price of the vehicle but also the interest rate, it helps to have good credit when leasing. And, a poor driving record of accidents and driving violations may inordinately drive up auto insurance costs with a leased vehicle.

Pay Cash or Finance Your Vehicle?

As in leasing, my approach to paying cash or financing would have been different 15 years ago. It used to go something like this: If you can pay for something with cash, do it. The elimination of a monthly payment will save you interest expense, reduce stress, and perhaps allow you to invest in savings what you eliminate in monthly payments.

Now, enter the year 2020. Interest rates are historically low for borrowers and many auto manufacturers are offering near zero interest rate deals through their lending agencies. It is difficult for me to argue with a client *not* to take such an offer.

However: I do not like financing a vehicle if there is poor credit resulting in an exorbitant interest rate. I also don't like financing if it is going to give you the false comfort to buy a higher price car that you really can't afford. Finally, I don't like car payment plans that go beyond four years. I know a four-year loan term is almost the exception rather than the rule these days, but every time I hear somebody talk about a seven-year payment plan I visibly cringe. If you're making payments on a car that you will own, get them done and over with as soon as possible so that you can eventually enjoy some payment-free months in a car that can still roll down the road.

Credit scores are an important part of our activities related to the rates we pay on all areas of debt, and autos are not exception. Even missing a $50 annual fee on one of your credit cards in a given month can drop a score between 50 and 100 points. On the other hand, financing a vehicle is one of the easiest and quickest ways to build or reestablish credit scores. After a year to eighteen months of on-time payments, your score could jump between 100 and 130 points—if all other debt payments are timely, too.

Having said all that, I also know the reality for many buying a car. They need a car today, not next week, their credit is lousy, and there's very little cash, if any, for a down payment. In these cases, you're at the mercy of a good finance manager to get you into a decent car—and be grateful for his or her help.

Negotiation Without High Anxiety

Here are a few tips that may make the buying process we all dread a little easier:

1. Prepare, prepare, prepare. Before you walk onto a lot or communicate on a website, check out car valuation resources, including Consumer Reports, Edmonds and Kelly Blue Book to determine what a fair price is for the car you want. Use this as a basis, but when making your first offer to the salesperson, start at least 10% below this figure. Tell her you've researched the price and you have quotes from other dealers.
2. Negotiate the price of the vehicle you plan to acquire before you negotiate your trade-in. Yes, these are two separate negotiations and you can get burned on both. Again, know the wholesale value of your car before walking on the lot. Dealers make more profit on trade-ins than on selling new cars.
3. Negotiate the price of the new vehicle and your trade-in before talking about monthly payments. Every auto salesman I've ever heard asks the following question after he shakes your hand: *What were you looking for in a monthly payment?* Answer: *I'm looking for a fair price and we can talk about the monthly payment later.*
4. Often, you can get better offers on the extras at a later date. These include extended warranties and other maintenance offers the finance manager will discuss with you.
5. Give the salesman a time limit. Something like, *I have to take my son to see his probation officer at 3:30.* Sales people love to wear the buyer down by repeated trips to the sales manager's office, phone calls to the garage to talk about your trade-in, and supposed negotiations with the bank to help finance you. I had one deal in which I did not leave the dealership until 11:30—at night! At this point my head was spinning, I

was exhausted, and I probably would have settled for a car with bald tires. And maybe I did.

6. Before arriving at the dealership, call the bank that you typically do business with and ask for a preapproved loan and find out what interest rate they will charge. This may be better than what the dealer offers, and even if it is not, you can use it as a negotiating tool.
7. Take a tablet and pencil with you so that you can continually write down the maze of figures they're throwing at you. Remember, no deal is finished until you sign the contract in the finance manager's office. Always be asking for an out-the-door price, which includes any miscellaneous fees, taxes, and warranties they add to what you are buying.
8. Regardless of what the salesperson and finance manager may tell you, manufacturer rebates are not contingent on the price you negotiate at your local dealer. Tip: It's usually better to take the rebate over the zero or lower interest rate offered.
9. Many people these days prefer to buy pre-owned vehicles from large retail chains that promise low price and no negotiation. As you shop online or visit locations, there is still no substitute for verifying fair current prices for the vehicle you are considering. Auto valuation resource Edmunds calls this value the TMV or true market value. Yes, we have initials for almost everything these days.

Now that wasn't so bad, was it?

Three Critical Takeaways from Chapter

1. Do your homework before you begin the purchase process.
2. Cars depreciate quickly. Do not fool yourself into believing that the vehicle is an investment.
3. When acquiring a car, an appropriate strategy for one person may not be best for somebody else.

Chapter 12

Income Tax Planning for Idiots—and Geniuses

Three Great Myths

1. Taxes greatly reduce how much one can save and invest during a lifetime.
2. Mortgage interest, property tax payments, and charitable donations generally reduce income taxes.
3. All income is taxed the same, so it is not important the type of income one has.

This chapter will be shorter than it would have been a few years ago before tax law changes occurred in 2018. IRS data suggest that more than 85% of you will *no longer* be deducting things like mortgage interest, taxes, charity, and medical expenses, because the total of these does not exceed the new higher standard deduction amounts allowed in the new tax code.

Even with some of these simplifications, taxes are still overly complicated, as illustrated in the chapter on the dizzying array of different IRA accounts.

Let's get into some of the nuts and bolts of income taxes and try to save some money.

Tax Deductions from Income

If our actual living expenses, such as property taxes, mortgage interest, and medical expenses do not exceed what the law provides as a standard deduction, we will just use the standard deduction amount and not bother adding up how much we spent for such things as pharmaceutical drugs, hearing aids, property taxes, mortgage interest, and donations to church and Goodwill. This is why approximately only 15% of taxpayers these days will report their actual itemized deductions.

Here are the 2024 standard deduction amounts for taxpayers who are:

Single	$14,600
Married Couple	$29,200
Head of household	$21,900

In addition to these amounts, if you are over 65 or blind, add $1,550. Therefore, a married couple, both over 65, and both legally blind, will have a standard deduction of $32,300 (29,200 + 1,550 + 1,550)

Here is a list of the most common expenses that we put into the bucket to determine if we exceed our standard deduction:

1. Medical expenses actually paid or charged to your credit card: health insurance, prescribed drugs, doctors, prescribed eye care, long term care insurance premiums, medical equipment, mileage to seek medical care, dentists, hearing aids, nursing home costs.

   Medical expenses not included are over-the-counter drugs, vitamins, and prescribed house fixtures for medical purposes that *add value* to your house, such as a pool for exercising those kinks out of your back.

   After we total our medical expenses, we may deduct only the amount that exceeds 10% of our income. This threshold prevents most of us from deducting medical costs.

2. Certain taxes actually paid during the year such as real estate property taxes, ad valorem auto tax, state income taxes, and in some cases, state sales tax. Under new rules, we can only deduct up to $10,000 per year in this category.

3. Mortgage interest on our home and second home, including a boat or RV if they have a kitchen and bathroom. We can

no longer deduct interest on home equity loans if the loans are not used to improve our homes.

4. Charitable contributions of money or items. They must be given to qualified charities such as a church or Goodwill. Giving your couch to your daughter is not a charitable contribution. Charitable contributions are limited to 60% of your income, which is not a problem for most people. If you exceed 60%, you can roll over the excess for five years.
5. Gambling expenses up to the amount of gambling income.

Let me list some of the items that in the past were included as itemized deductions, but under the new tax rules, are <u>not</u>. They may surprise you.

1. Unreimbursed job expenses if you are an employee
2. Job search expenses
3. Tax preparation fees
4. Investment management fees and expenses
5. Casualty losses, such as, for car accidents or home disasters, except if the casualty occurred in an area declared a national disaster area.

Other <u>Non-deductible</u> Expenses I Get Asked About Often

1. Funeral expenses
2. Medical marijuana
3. Medical expenses paid for a non-dependent such as a girlfriend or a grown independent child
4. Life insurance premiums
5. Interest expense on credit cards and car loans
6. Gifts to friends or relatives
7. Your personal cell phone or computer used for your employment

8. Virtually all closing costs on the purchase of a residential house except for so-called bank closing mortgage points
9. Home improvements (excluding some energy-saving improvements—see below)

Now you may understand why only 15% of taxpayers itemize deductions.

Tax Tip to Itemize - For those of us who have deductions of actual expenses that, when added together, get close to the standard deduction, the strategy I often suggest is one of clustering or bunching as many of your expenses into one year so you can try to itemize every other year. For instance, instead of donating evenly to your church, donate heavily every other year. If you can time your property taxes, bunched them in alternative years similar to your charitable deductions. If you have a big dental procedure due, try to time it, as difficult as that may seem, so that you pay for it in the same year that you are paying your property taxes and heavy charitable deductions.

To easily remember which year you are bunching expenses, identify yourself as an odd year or even year person (perhaps your year of birth) and write this on your tax file. Then you will always and automatically know for which year you're trying to bunch expenses.

Tax Tip on most common itemized deduction missed – Mileage. Even though unreimbursed mileage for employees is no longer deductible, mileage for driving to medical offices and hospitals still is. Mileage to perform charitable services, such as driving to volunteer at an American Cancer Society fundraiser, is deductible, as well as driving to Goodwill to deliver that tired sofa. Sorry, but weekly driving to church or temple is not deductible.

<u>Tax Tip to deduct Charitable Expenses if not itemizing</u> - If you are over age 70½, and have an IRA, you are allowed to ask your IRA custodian (broker, bank) to directly pay the charity from your IRA account. You can then exclude this amount from your IRA income, and this same amount goes toward satisfying the total that you are required to withdraw annually. This tax break is called Qualified Charitable Distribution or QCD. (Congress cancelled required distributions for 2020 due to the virus and thus there is no need to do an IRA Qualified Charitable Distribution.)

Tax Tip to Receive Income Taxed at Lower Rates—or Not at All

You may not have realized that not all income is treated equally. Because of incentives and conventions in the tax code, various types of income are taxed differently. You should know about these rules because they may influence how you invest.

<u>Dividend Income</u> - Dividend income from normal common stocks and stock funds is taxed at lower rates than, say, working income and typical interest income. Such dividends are called qualified dividends. In fact, for most taxpayers, dividend income is taxed at a zero rate. Dividends only become taxable if your income rises to the 22% tax rate level, and then it still gets a discounted rate, 15%. If you're a really big hitter with income exceeding approximately $434,000 ($489,000 if married), then the maximum rate is only 23.4%.

To put this in perspective, if I own $10,000 worth of ATT stock and am receiving my 5% (a close approximation) dividend of $500, and I am in the 12% tax bracket—typical of most Americans—I pay no tax on that income. Zero, zilch. At the same time, my neighbor has a $10,000 CD for which he receives 1.0% bank interest of $100, also a true approximation. If he is in the same 12% bracket as I, he will receive $100 interest income and pay $12 in taxes, netting $88. I will receive $500 income and pay no tax. What a country!

Be careful in thinking that all income called dividends gets a break. Interest from bonds inside bond mutual funds is *called* dividends, but it does not get favored dividend tax treatment. Nor do most dividends from Real Estate Investment Trusts (REITS).

Capital Gain Income - In simplest terms, capital gains result when a taxpayer sells an asset, such as a security or real estate, for more than it costs. The good news: capital gains get the same favored treatment as common stock dividends. The bad news, sort of: In order to qualify, the asset must be held at least a year plus one day. This should not be difficult for most investors, especially since short-term trading is often not advised.

Preferred Stock income - Dividends from preferred stock are usually treated as tax favored qualified dividends. That's good, because preferred stocks are usually very good income producers with more stable values than common stocks. I prefer to buy preferred stock funds more than individual preferred but note that preferred funds that include REITs will have dividends that are not qualified.

REIT income - Real Estate Investment Trust income does not get favorable dividend treatment but may get a break under the new tax code for reducing business income tax rates. This is called qualified business income or QBI. So, when you find a good REIT security or fund, you'll receive good income and probably a 20% discount in taxes.

Municipal Bond Income - When states and local municipalities borrow money, they pay interest, but the interest has always been wonderfully exempt from federal income. Nice. This tax-free feature usually allows municipalities to pay lower interest rates in the marketplace than comparable borrowers, so it is not automatically advantageous to the investor unless the investor is in a higher tax bracket. Having said that, I know people in a low tax bracket who buy muni bonds just because they hate paying taxes. Buy individual municipal bonds if you know what you're doing; otherwise, consider municipal bond *funds*. (Note: Municipal bond interest may be subject to state income tax.)

Social Security Benefits - For many taxpayers, social security income is tax-free income. The formula for determining if it is or not goes something like this: Add half of your social security income to your other income, including tax exempt municipal income, and if the total exceeds $25,000, then Social Security *begins* to become taxable. That's if you're single. If married, use $32,000 instead of $25,000. The problem with social security benefits is that one year it may be tax-free for you, but in another year, when you have more "other" income, social security suddenly becomes taxable. That can be an ugly year. The taxpayer is, one, paying tax on the other income, two, paying tax on a portion of social security, and three, the combination of the first two puts the unfortunate soul in a higher tax bracket. I call it the triple whammy. Strategy if possible: Spread that other income over more than one year to reduce creating taxable social security.

The moral of the story for investing with regards to taxation: Not all income is taxed the same. Consideration of tax consequences for various types of investments is critical, especially over the long-term. Please consult a tax expert, such as a CPA, to develop your individual strategy.

Tips to Minimize Retirement Income Taxation

Having just said that not all income is taxed the same, one type of income is: distributions from traditional IRA and 401(k) accounts. Withdrawals from these accounts are all taxed at regular income tax rates, identical to work income. The good news, however, is that dividends and capital gains inside IRAs and 401(k)s are not taxed at all—until they are distributed out of the account to you. This makes strategizing about what to own and sell inside these accounts easier. If the security in the IRA account produces what would be normally taxable income, we don't care as long as it stays *inside* the IRA. And if I buy REITS, which usually produce good income but do not qualify as tax-exempt or qualified dividends, it doesn't matter because all of this income is sheltered inside the retirement IRA or 401(k) account.

By taking advantage of the tax shelter that retirement accounts provide, we can load them with securities that produce lots of income, as opposed to growth securities that are hoped to appreciate but pay little or no annual dividend or interest.

Similarly, if we have an IRA capital loss from a sale in more volatile growth securities, we can-not deduct the loss. However, If the same security is held in a non-retirement account, we can deduct the loss.

In short, if we have a choice, we'd rather put income-producing securities more in retirement (IRA, etc.) accounts, and growth investments, such as high-flying stocks and stock funds, in non-retirement accounts.

A comment I frequently hear from salesmen pushing various financial products, usually annuities, is that the normal person is significantly hurt in their efforts to save for retirement because of special tax laws. The same salesperson claims that their product avoids these problems. Annuity salespeople claim their product will avoid or defer income taxes and therefore allow a more comfortable retirement. Nonsense. People don't have enough in retirement savings, not because of taxation, but, because they did not save enough during their younger years. And this is coming from a CPA and investment advisor who ran a tax planning firm for 25 years.

Tax Tip for Residential Renewable Energy Tax Credits

Politicians keep threatening to end this program, but it has been extended through 2032. Remember, tax credits reduce actual tax due, unlike typical deductions that reduce taxable income. That's good. Unfortunately, most of the credits for things we commonly buy to improve our residence and increase energy efficiency are capped at a total of $1,200.

Here are some highlights . . .

Energy Efficient Home Improvement Credit. For 2023 through 2032, there is a credit of 30% of the cost up to a maximum of $1,200 (no lifetime limit) for:

- Exterior doors, windows, skylight and insulation materials
- Central air conditioners, water heaters, furnaces, boilers and heat pumps
- Biomass stoves and boilers
- Home energy audits

Residential Clean Energy Credit. For 2023 through 2032, there is a credit of 30% of the cost, with no annual or lifetime maximum:

- Solar, wind, and geothermal power generation
- Solar water heaters
- Fuel cells
- Battery Storage

Electric Vehicle Credit. There is a maze of rules and regulations for this category. Rather than providing possibly out-of-date information, I suggest that you check tax regulations for your specific auto and date of purchase.

Tax Tip for Filing Married, Filing Jointly or Married Filing Separately

Let's talk about an issue I get questions about often. Married couples commonly ask if they should file separately to save taxes. Probably not, but each situation is different, and you need to pump the numbers into the computer to be sure.

First, remember that it is illegal to file as a single or head-of-household person if you are legally married. Conversely, if you are single, it is against the law to file as married. If indeed you are legally married, there are only two choices: married filing jointly or married filing separately.

The architects of the tax code will want to tell you that they have made the rules neutral so that it doesn't matter whether you file jointly or separately. Not quite true. There are "penalties" for filing separately, including the loss of some child credits for younger taxpayers, and for seniors, the amount of taxation on social security income. Even though I describe these gotchas as penalties, the IRS would say, probably correctly, that they are necessary so that people do not take advantage of tax breaks.

As it turns out, most taxpayers I know who have filed separately do not do it to save taxes, but rather to protect one of the partners. Perhaps one spouse is behind in child support payments or one spouse does not want to be affiliated with the other's business activities. And of course, if the couple is proceeding through a divorce, and at each other's throats, filing separately is often chosen.

Bottom line: Crank the numbers both ways to be sure. If you think being legally single might be a better long-term tax strategy, see chapter 9.

Tax Tip if You are Single but Living With Partner and Their Child(ren)

In this age of blended families, singles living with each other, and unofficial parents taking care of kids, the rules for who can claim whom and what the filing status is leaves everyone scratching their heads. One of the reasons for the confusion is that the new tax rules eliminate deducting dependents as exemptions on our tax returns. If we can't deduct exemptions, is having a dependent still important for filing a tax return?

You bet it is.

First, if you are legally single on December 31, you get a tax break if you can file as head of household when other people are living with you. If you are head of household, there is a higher standard deduction and more favorable tax rates. That's good. But the deal breaker for most of us is that the other person in the house must be a legal relative to you, like a child, mother, or father-in-law. He can't be your girlfriend or her son unless you legally marry your girlfriend or adopt the child. You must also provide more than half of the support for this other person, and if your biological minor child or college age student, they must have lived with you for more than six months of the year.

Believe it or not, as long as you provide more than 50% care for a parent, they don't have to live with you to be a dependent, which for some of you, may make you very happy.

So now, we generally know whether we can file head of household and get lower tax rates.

But we also want to get other perks from having or caring for a child, especially all those tax credits that directly reduce our taxes and increase our refund, such as the Earned Income Credit, the Child Tax Credit, the Child and Dependent Care Credit (for daycare and babysitting), and higher Education Credits. Yes, we have credits coming out our ears related to kids. And each has its own encyclopedia of rules and restrictions.

So, let's return to the unmarried couple living together with a child. How do we get all these juicy credits on our tax return that could be several thousand dollars?

The IRS and congress have come up with something called a qualifying child. If you have a qualifying child, you may be eligible for tax credits. Requirements:

1. The child (or descendent) must be a blood relative or legally adopted child of the taxpayer. Yes, this immediately eliminates your boyfriend's or girlfriend's kids.
2. The child must live with the taxpayer for more than half the year. Exceptions: divorced parents, birth or death during the year, and yes, don't forget, kidnapped children.
3. The child must be under 19 years of age at the end of the year or under 24 if a full-time student for at least five months of the year. A disabled child may be any age.
4. The child did not provide more than half of his or her own financial support during the year.

From these rules you can see that if two adults live together, only the natural parent of the child can take advantage of those nice benefits like earned income credit and child credits.

However, there is another rule that gives us a little break. You may qualify for a $500 tax credit, that is, an amount that comes directly off your tax due, if you have what they call a "qualified dependent." It's a little easier to meet this requirement than qualifying child status. First, the person does not have to be your blood relative, but they must have lived with you for the entire year. They also can't claim themselves on their own return or on another person's return. Finally, having a qualified dependent does not qualify the adult to file as head of household, which would have lowered taxes more.

Therefore, a person not married but living with their partner and their partner's child cannot claim head of household status but can claim the other qualified dependent status for those that live with him or her full-time, if the child does not file her own return, and the child's work income is less than $12,500 (in 2023), and the child is not included on anybody else's tax return. There are lots of "ands" on this list to get the $500 tax savings, but it's better than nothing.

The $500 credit is also a nice benefit for people who are taking care of adult relatives such as a sister, uncle or parent, that the taxpayer supports, or for the dependent with little or no income. (And good news, social security income of the dependent does not count against the $12,500 income max in this equation.)

Because child tax credits and earned income credits are typically worth much more than the $500 "other dependent" credit, the natural parent of the child rather than the parent's boyfriend or girlfriend should file a tax return and claim his or her own child. Crank the numbers and consult a professional to find the preferred path.

Tax Tip: The Government Will Help You Pay Your Health Insurance if You are Even Close to Being in a Low-Income Category.

Under current tax law, if you meet low income requirements and have no other insurance, such as Medicare or coverage from your employer, Uncle Sam will help pay part or almost all of your health insurance. This is commonly called Obamacare, but officially named the Patient Protection and Affordable Care Act. It has not gone away under President Trump and the essence of Obamacare probably never will, now that we are accustomed to having it.

The way it works: For those of us not covered by other insurance plans, we go into the federal healthcare marketplace at www.healthcare.gov. There, we enter income and family information, then choose a plan. Based on our estimated income, the system or website will tell us what our net premium is. The lower our income, the more subsidy we receive from the government, and the lower our own net out-of-pocket cost.

Here's the trick, however. If we understate our estimated income, then we receive too much subsidy, which we have to pay back when we file our tax return the following year.

But here is what nobody is telling you: As long as your income is no more than four times the poverty level for your family size, the government kindly limits how much you have to pay back. It varies from $350 to $3,000 depending on tax filing status and income level. In these days when the annual cost of health insurance can easily exceed $10,000, having to pay only $3.000 for health insurance if you underestimated income is a really good deal. You will owe this deficit when filing your tax return. And, if you normally get a nice refund, the underpayment is simply deducted from the refund, meaning that you don't even have to write a check.

The bottom line: It is far better to underestimate your income then to overestimate it.

A note to the people who underestimate their income, but then sneak over the income level which exceeds four times the poverty rate. If you are in this unfortunate category, you receive no subsidy and the amount you owe is not limited to $3,000. You are stuck for the entire subsidy that Obamacare advanced to you. For single people with no dependents, this income level is $51,040, equal to four times the poverty level. The level then goes up as your family expands as shown on the following chart:

2024 4X Poverty Guideline Amounts

Persons in Family/Household	4X Poverty $
1	$60,240
2	$81,760

3	$103,280
4	$124,800
5	$146,320
6	$167,840
7	$210,880

A note about Obamacare plans: If you are young and healthy, say under 35 years of age, it is often more economical to get a health insurance plan outside of the government marketplace. You may find lower deductibles and even lower premiums. This is especially true if you won't qualify for government subsidies to help with premiums because your income is too high.

Finally, Obamacare rules differ by state. In Florida, for instance, you must have earned income (or alimony income), in essence, be working, to participate. This is not true, however, in many other states.

Three Critical Takeaways from Chapter

1. About half of adults pay no income tax and only 15% deduct itemized deductions, such as, charity, mortgage interest, and medical expenses.
2. Various investments come with different tax rates and consequences. Do your homework before making the plunge.
3. Tax laws are a mess. Seek professional help.

Chapter 13

Rental Property—Becoming a Landlord

Three Great Myths

1. The price of the property is less important than rents charged tenants.
2. Smaller rent can be charged if the investor has no mortgage on the property.
3. There are good tax breaks for owning rental property.

Over the years, I have worked with dozens of clients who have managed rental property and, indeed, I continue to be a landlord myself. Like any other investment, it comes with risks, rewards, and occasional headaches—major headaches.

Some Tips if You are Considering Such a Venture.

1. Buy cheap. The most successful investors and landlords I know have a knack for buying their properties at an exceptionally low price. This is absolutely, positively the most important ingredient in owning successful rental property. It is not the tenants you'll find; it is not the rent you can charge; it is not even the potential appreciation you may realize. The first step is to get a good buy on your purchase price. This factor is so important because the rents you charge and your overhead cost structure will almost be predetermined based on the nature of the property and its location. Do not think that if you overpay for a house you can make up for it later with higher rents or that hoped for appreciation. Your ego may tell you that I am wrong, but through 30 years of experience watching people suffer through lousy decisions and preparing their tax returns, you must believe me on this one.

Strategies to get a good price include buying fixer-uppers, seeking out foreclosures, or buying during economic dips when house prices fall. I've seen successful rental investors who are real estate agents and title attorneys, because they have more inside information on which houses are selling and also those that are good values. Unfortunately, most of us don't have these tools available to us.

2. Be able to charge enough rent. Know your market. One of the biggest shortcomings I see with landlords is that they do not charge enough rent to make their investment economically favorable. This may be because they pay too much for the house or because the local markets do not allow sufficient rental rate levels, or they are afraid to upset their tenant.

In Florida, one of the rules I like to tell clients about is the one percent rule. A landlord should be able to collect 1% of the price he paid for the property in rents each month. That is, if the market value is $100,000 for a rental property, you should be able to collect close to 1% or $1,000 each month for rent. With current low interest rates, an owner can get away with collecting 0.8%, but even that is cutting it close. This level of rent income is needed to cover the landlord's profit in addition to costs, including property taxes, maintenance and repairs, insurance, and other surprise expenses.

Clients have often responded to this 1% rule by saying that it does not apply to them because they have no mortgage, and therefore, according to them, their overhead structure is much lower. Not true. If they paid cash for the house, they are tying up their own money, which could have been invested somewhere else.

More bad news: if the property has homeowner dues or other special assessments, they should be added to the 1%.

I have found that the one percent rule may not apply to every location. In Southern California, for instance, it is more like a 0.3% rule. The apparent reason that rents are low compared to real estate values is somewhat unique to Southern California where property values have skyrocketed. The result is that owners have found it easier to get a mortgage loan to escalate the price of real estate for ownership, while renters still have difficulty making ends meet. This has compressed rental rates even in areas that are not rent controlled. Lesson: Owning rental properties in very attractive areas may not produce attractive profits.

3. See an attorney before you get too deep. Attorneys, especially ones that focus on real estate, can give you a reality check on the property that you're buying: it's location, the purchase contract, and of course the written leasing agreement you'll need with your tenant. A few hundred, or even several hundred, dollars to pay for these services and feedback are well worth it and may be one of the most important investments you will ever make.

4. Screen tenants carefully. I could fill another book with nightmare tenant stories. Drug addicts, criminals, domestic abusers, chronically late payers, and fly-by-night losers would comprise the chapters. There are websites available to help you screen tenants' backgrounds. For a small fee and after you have sent them a copy of the tenant application, these website companies will send you information about the applicant that is invaluable. Realize, however, that most tenants come with issues such as previous bankruptcies, perhaps an arrest here or there, and inconsistent job history. If they were perfect, they would not need your lousy rental property.

After research and a check of their background, use your gut. A hypothetical question you might ask yourself is whether you would hire that person to work for you. You don't want to discriminate with regards to race, age, religion. The requirement of essentially three months' rent upfront, that is, the first month, last month, and a security deposit for damage, will screen out many applicants. That's a lot of cash to get together for most tenants.

5. Reside near your rental property. As tenants come and go and repair issues come up, you need to be close by to monitor what is happening. Even if you have excellent contractors at hand to fix the air conditioner or to repair a leaky pipe, monitoring and supervising this process is much more difficult if you live a thousand miles away.

6. Inspect property regularly. Even when I have wonderful tenants, I still show my face several times a year for an inspection. I give them 24 hours' notice to clean up the place, but I advise them that when I arrive, I'm going to make a quick walk through the dwelling. This visit also ends up being a good public relations activity because it gives you and the tenant a chance to stay on good terms and communicate about repair issues and the overall condition of the property. Obviously, this task is difficult to carry out regularly if you're not residing near your rental property.

7. Raise your rent at renewal. Too many clients and friends I've known who are landlords tell me, almost brag, that they've charged the same rent to the tenant for the last 15 years. This is insane. The cost of everything goes up over time and so must your rent. Pick a reasonable rate and consult with your attorney about how to incorporate it in the lease, but make sure you don't forget to make it a structured component of your investment process.

8. Be a handyman. Or know a good one who is willing to work for you when you call them. Beside buying properties for a bargain, the most successful landlords I know are very handy with fixing things around their properties. They don't need a handyman and therefore avoid much of this expense. If you have never picked up a hammer or do not have a network of people you can call to help repair things around your property, your landlord life could get complicated—and expensive—real quickly. I am a bit lucky in this department, because over the years I've become friends with some very good craftsmen, including a plumber, an air conditioner repairman, and a skilled handyman. When a tenant calls on a Sunday night at 10 o'clock to complain that the air conditioner is not working, it's now my problem. If I don't have a trusted technician that I can call, my stress level just multiplied by five.

9. Examine rental rules in your state. Speaking of stress, states vary about their rules regarding landlords dealing with tenants, specifically, eviction rules. For example, Florida is considered landlord friendly, while Maryland is not. In states unfriendly to landlords, the renter may be able to stay in property several months after receiving an eviction notice for nonpayment of rent.

Other Things to Expect as a Landlord

1. Expect the unexpected. You may think you're just a property investor but as a landlord you may become a life coach for your tenants. Often the trials and tribulations of their lives affect the property they live in and the rent they pay you.

2. Repairs and Maintenance never end. Just as the Golden Gate Bridge must be painted constantly to avoid crumbling into the bay, so too does your rental property require maintenance. And it's just not painting. There may be new roofs, lawn care, carpet, heating units, and the list goes on. If this process is too stressful for you, reconsider rental property as an investment.
3. Rewards are long term. Owning rental property is by no means a get-rich-quick endeavor. Over time real estate market prices go up and then down and back up again; major repairs may eat up what you thought was last year's profit; and, your property may go several months without any tenants at all and therefore provide no rental income or cash flow.
4. Income tax benefits are overrated. The only free deduction landlords get is the one for depreciation expense. Every other cost is a deduction because you laid out good hard cash for it. And if you're in the 22% tax bracket, for instance, Uncle Sam may be subsidizing 22% of that cost, but the rest of it falls on your shoulders. This means you must track and document all of your expenses related to the rental, including travel to the property and completing associated errands.

Here's more bad news related to passive loss tax rules: If the income on your tax return exceeds $150,000, you may not be able to take any net loss on your rental property that year. Instead, you will have to carry that loss over to a future year when either your income drops below $150,000, you sell the property, or you have net rental income profit.

Here's even more bad news: Remember that nice depreciation expense I just talked about as a deduction? Well, when you eventually sell the rental property, you have to add back depreciation expense as income, which increases your taxable gain.

Three Critical Takeaways from Chapter

1. Buying the right property at the right price is the most important component of managing a successful rental investment.
2. Seek legal and accounting advice *before* you make too many blunders.
3. Owning rental property is not for everyone, but many landlords love it.

Chapter 14

Credit and Identity Protection—Without Costs

Three Great Myths

1. Credit protection companies protect your credit.
2. Identity theft happens if someone inappropriately uses your credit card.
3. It costs money to protect your identity.

Don't Let Crooks Steal Your Identity!

We have all heard about the terrible hacking stories of bad people getting into private databases at Target Stores and Yahoo. With all this apparent vulnerability, just how do we protect our identity so we don't wake up to find that somebody in Miami just bought a lawnmower at The Home Depot in our name? (Yes, that actually happened to me several years ago.)

There are basically three areas in our financial identity that are exposed to risk of fraud:

1. Someone <u>stealing your credit card</u> or using your card information to purchase things on your account.

2. Someone <u>stealing your personal information</u> and then getting a new credit *account* for themselves to borrow money or make a purchase, like a car or new phone—or new lawnmower.

3. Someone filing a tax return in your name to the IRS after they have somehow obtained your personal information. The IRS ends up sending a bogus tax refund to the crook.

Some remedies for each of these:

1. A Crook Stealing or Using Your Credit Card – Fortunately, the credit card companies and banks that issue cards have become very good at detecting unusual and fraudulent charges based on your historical behavior. They will often call or notify you if they suspect a problem—or may just reject the charge.

Also, for those of you with smart cell phones, I strongly suggest you sign up for a service (i.e., get a free phone app) in which the credit card company immediately notifies you in a text message after every use of the card, so you, the user, have up-to-the-minute tracking of all charge transactions. I have this service, it is excellent, and it is more effective than a monitoring service that bills you monthly fees.

Fraudulent use of credit cards—believe it or not, perpetrated by friends and family, too—is another reason to have fewer rather than more of them. If you insist on having 25 cards, one for each department store, airline, and gas station, leave as many of them as possible home when you are out and about, and certainly when long-distance traveling.

Another tip: Fraud activity using a credit card typically has less impact on our lives than fraud involving a debit card, which is tied to our checking account. Accordingly, experts tell us to use our credit more than debit cards if there is any fear of shenanigans happening.

2. A Crook Stealing Your Personal Information to Get New Credit in Your Name - Credit monitoring services keep a check on people accessing your credit, but unfortunately, it can be a little too late, like closing the stable door *after* the horse has bolted and left the barn. Credit monitoring services charge a fee to help you try to fix the problem *after* it has occurred.

An alternative to a credit monitoring service is to request that credit agencies freeze access to your credit. This locks the stable door so that the horse can't get out in the first place. This is a good idea for people who are not getting lots of new loans, but, even if you do need to get a new loan, you can easily do a temporary unfreeze. I happen to have this in place for me and it works great. And it's free.

The three credit reporting agencies you need to contact to freeze your credit are: Experian, TransUnion, and Equifax. When you visit their websites be sure to go to their credit freeze section, which is free. Their sites often attempt to divert you to their monitoring services, where they charge you monthly fees.

3. A Crook Filing a Tax Return in Your Name – Unfortunately, a credit monitoring service or even the freezing of your credit can *not* prevent this fraud. Whenever you provide your personal information to someone or an organization, such as your doctor's office, a clerk in the office can hand your information over to her cousin who uses it to file a tax return in your name, and fudge (a technical term!) the numbers so that a refund is sent to his house, not yours.

The only way the average person can prevent this is to attempt to file the tax return early before the crook files. As a note, if this fraud does happen, the IRS works to correct the situation, and issues a special PIN (Personal I.D. password number) to the taxpayer for future tax filings. Bottom line: Try to file early to avoid all this hassle.

Following the three cost-free prevention steps above will greatly reduce the risk of someone stealing your identity and turning your financial life upside down.

Other Things Crooks Can Do

There are other areas in which fraud enters our lives to cause havoc. Here is a short list with which all of us should be familiar and alert:

1. Phone calls from the IRS. By now, most of us—yes, even I—have received fake calls from scammers pretending to be the IRS threatening lawsuits and even arrest. 999 times out of 1000, the IRS will NOT call, but instead write. Do not give the caller any information.

Tip: Tell them to write to you with their notice.

2. Phone calls from distressed grandchildren. Yes, people pretend to be your grandchild calling in need of money to stay out of jail or to fly back into the country after being stranded. I know, it sounds crazy, but sometimes it works, especially with elderly grandparents who may not talk to their families often.

Tip: Tell the grandkids to call their *parents*!

3. Phone calls or letters promising big wins, like a lottery or raffle. Yes, I personally know a retiree who wanted to provide more money for her heirs, so she agreed to buy raffles from an unknown caller for a chance to win big bucks. Fifty thousand dollars of lost money later, the family is still wondering how it all happened.

Tip: Buy a lottery ticket at the 7-11 store instead.

4. Fraudulent emails contaminating your computer. Crooks, called hackers in computer lingo, love to send out emails to you fishing for personal information and ruining your computer. They're so smart, they make the emails look like they come from people you know. And everybody is vulnerable.

Tip: Carefully review the subject and source of emails before opening. Also, make sure that you have anti-virus software on your computer. Finally, some cell phones, especially those of Apple, have good built-in security for preventing viruses, so think about opening email on the phone instead of your computer.

5. Domestic workers who want to do more than clean the house. Many retirees have home health care givers who can be very friendly and helpful, but also fraudulent.

Tip: If they start paying more attention to your checkbook than to vacuuming, be careful.

6. If you have a relative or friend who is aging, he or she may be more vulnerable to any or all of the above, so try to keep a closer eye on their financial transactions, like ATM withdrawals, bank statements, and telephone calls.

Tip: Most important, any time you have a doubt or suspicion about something fishy, please call your tax professional, a relative, or another trusted person in your life. The crooks love it when you tell *no one*.

Three Critical Takeaways from Chapter

1. You can't protect your privacy, so protect your identity: Get a credit freeze!
2. If you have an elder parent, review this chapter with them.
3. Communicate with familiar advisors or family members before committing financially to *anything*.

Part Three

HEADING INTO THE SENIOR YEARS

Chapter 15

Social Security Planning Summed Up: Live Long

Three Great Myths

1. If you wait longer to start receiving social security income, your overall lifetime benefits will be higher.
2. If you stop earning income a few years before you start collecting social security, it significantly reduces benefits later.
3. You're likely to increase social security benefits if you marry.

Each of these chapters could be an entire book on its own, and Social Security planning is no exception. This chapter will not delve into Social Security disability issues but rather focus on planning for old age Social Security income benefits.

Here's what we'll discuss:

- Appropriate age to start collecting benefits
- Strategies for married, and divorced people
- Strategies for widows and widowers

Appropriate Age to Start Collecting Benefits:

Most of us know the general theme of Social Security retirement benefits: the older you start collecting, the higher the monthly amount. You can typically start receiving benefits at 62; rising monthly income amounts cap out at age 70. The midpoint of the range is called Full Retirement Age, between ages 66 and 67, depending upon when you were born.

For illustration purposes, if we assume a calculated midpoint monthly income benefit of $1,600 at age 67, the following illustrates the range of monthly incomes you receive by choosing various ages to *start* benefits:

Age	Monthly Benefit
62	$1,120
63	$1,200
64	$1,280
65	$1,386
66	$1,493
67	$1,600
68	$1,728
69	$1,856
70	$1,984

If you delay the commencement of payments from age 62 until 70, the monthly payments at the later age are a whopping 77% higher. By using the figures above, the loss of that monthly $1,120 over eight years totals $107,520. For a lot of people, that is a lot of money. The person waiting to take benefits until 70 would have to live about another 10 years, to almost 80, collecting the higher income, in order to make up for the early payments not received.

Most retirees I know choose a middle ground for their Social Security income commencement date, electing to start benefits between 64 and 67. Besides small cost of living adjustments, once you choose a start date, you are locked into a benefit amount unless you can take advantage of a few spousal elections discussed below.

Also, little known, you have one year after starting benefits to change your mind about the start date, but you must repay all that you received. I have never seen anyone do this.

Let's face it, the selection of a start date is a crapshoot. Or as Clint Eastwood's Dirty Harry said, "You've got to ask yourself one question. Do I feel lucky?" If we delay benefits until 70, then die of cancer or a heart attack at age 69, we've just lost $107,520. Even if we make it to 70, we must live almost another 10 years just to break even. And at 80, are we too old to even enjoy this extra income we've waited so long for?

Using the figures above, if we delay benefits from age 62 to 67—the so-called full retirement age for those born after 1959—we give up $67,200 in benefits over those five years on the bet that we'll live long enough to more than overcome this sacrifice. However, even just delaying until age 67 results in a break-even period of approximately 12 years, age 79.

When analyzing start-date decisions with clients, the discussion must be very frank about other sources of income, lifestyle (e.g., obesity, smoking, drinking, extravagant spending, etc.), and of course, health issues, including mental health. It sounds presumptuous and cold, but often we develop a life expectancy chart. You should, too. If life after 80 is less likely, you may not want to delay benefits too long, if possible.

I have had clients claim that dementia is prevalent in their family, and since they don't expect to enjoy their life after 80, they refuse to delay benefits. However, another person in a similar situation chose to *defer* benefits with the thought that the extra income later in life would be needed for additional medical care.

Of course, many don't have an option to choose early benefits because they still need to work to make ends meet. If your 2020 work income exceeds $18,240 during the period you're under full retirement age, you will lose a good chunk of your benefits, anyway. If you happen to reach full retirement age in 2020, the limit on your earnings for the months *before* reaching full retirement age is $48,600. For those who just like to work and work, they may be the true lucky ones. By continuing to work far into their sixties and delaying Social Security benefits, their work income will probably exceed the social security income they delayed receiving; then later when retired, their scheduled monthly Social Security payments will be much higher.

Clients have asked whether working a few extra years and paying related social security taxes through wage withholdings will increase their benefits later. Probably not. That's because the complicated government formula to calculate your benefits is based on using average monthly earnings over your 35 highest-paid years of income (adjusted for inflation). Thus, if you get that part-time job driving for Uber to earn a few extra dollars at age 64, that income and the related social security taxes paid will probably not increase your benefits later. Accordingly, in light of the 35-year formula, it is difficult to increase—or decrease—benefits with factoring in just one or two years of additional work.

Strategies for Married Couples

For married couples to have interconnected benefits, they must be legally married at least one year. To collect interconnected benefits if divorced, the couple must have been married 10 years. But having said that, our benefits are first based on our own work history and when each of us chooses to start receiving social security income.

The interconnected benefit I refer to relates to what is referred to as spousal benefits. If married at least a year, spouse B may elect to receive half of the benefits coming to spouse A. The catch: Spouse A must already be eligible to receive benefits and Spouse B, the one who wants 50% of spouse A, must be at least age 62.

Choosing this strategy works well when the benefits A is receiving far exceed those to be received by B, say if B has been a stay-at-home parent or only worked part-time over the years. If it turns out that Spouse B applies for spousal benefits and his or her own benefits exceed more than 50% of the spouse's, she will not receive both, just the one that is higher.

Also, the 50%-of-benefits rule is fully 50% only if the electing lower income spouse (spouse B) can wait until her full retirement age, usually between 66 and 67. If you start earlier, you won't receive as much—for the rest of your life.

The other primary way benefits of spouses are connected (besides being divorced, which we will discuss below) is if one spouse dies, the survivor will receive the *greater* social security income of 1) their own or 2) their deceased spouse, but not both. And the Social Security income level is based on the income level at the time of death. So, if the decedent decided to take lower income at 62, that lower income level is what the survivor steps into when considering which of the spouse's benefits is greater.

Ideal strategy for married couples: From the rules I describe above, the optimum strategy may be pretty much common sense. The spouse with the higher expected benefits—due to higher career work income—should delay taking benefits with the goal to increase the monthly income received after one of them dies. Meanwhile, the spouse with the lower benefits should begin taking income sooner, even at 62. Why? Because when one of the spouses kicks the bucket, those lower benefits will stop, so if you don't take them now, you'll never get them, and deciding to defer this income will not help increase the eventual income from the other spouse's higher amount. With this strategy, it doesn't matter which spouse dies first.

This strategy of "spouse A delay and spouse B don't delay" still works if one spouse is deathly ill. With a married couple, if both live to 65, the odds are that *one* of them will live to age 90, so delaying one of the benefits makes sense in the long term.

However, this strategy probably won't work if *both* spouses are deathly ill. In that case, take both benefits as soon as possible.

Should an unmarried couple consider marriage just to maximize benefits? Perhaps, but only if one person's benefits significantly exceed the other's.

If you're thinking of marrying a terminally ill person with higher benefits just to latch on to spousal benefits, do not forget the one-year waiting period. Therefore, after walking down the aisle you must keep your new honey alive for 12 months before stepping into his or her benefits.

Divorced Strategies

If you divorce, you may use the spousal benefits rule described above to collect up to 50% of your former spouse's benefits, even if your ex-spouse has remarried. But you must have been married at least 10 years to do this. Not living together, not engaged, but legally married. And the amount is a full 50% only if you wait until *your* (not your ex's) full retirement age, which for most of us is between age 66 and 67. If you start earlier, you get less. Unfortunately, if your ex-spouse delays receiving benefits beyond full retirement age to receive a higher benefit, say to age 70, this increased amount does not spill over to you.

To collect from the earnings record of your former spouse, you must be at least 62 years of age and unmarried. For you to receive benefits, it's not necessary that your ex-spouse be actually collecting benefits, only that he or she be eligible to receive them.

What may sound strange is that the ex-spouses receiving this 50% from a particular person can number more than one, as long as each ex-spouse meets the 10-year minimum time rule. Even more strange, although you can only collect on one ex-spouse, it's one ex-spouse *at a time.* As you move through retirement years, it's possible to flip from one ex-spouse to another in order to maximize benefits.

The Social Security administration will automatically evaluate whether receiving the 50% ex-spousal benefit is greater than your own benefit amounts based on your *own* earnings.

A painful mistake I've seen is for spouses to get divorced before waiting the full 10-year marriage period. When I told one client about this strategy, she still refused to wait just a few months more to finalize the divorce because she hated the guy so much. It cost her thousands in benefits later, but I guess she thought it was worth it to be done with him.

The other common mistake is for the divorced person to remarry. When you remarry, the benefits of the first spouse go away. This is a big no-no if the first spouse made lots of money and neither you nor your new spouse do. (Note: It does not matter that the ex-spouse you are claiming against remarries. You are still entitled to 50% of that person's benefit.)

A clever strategy to pull off: If your number one spouse was a big earner, apply to collect 50% on his or her social security after you're divorced, then later remarry big income earner #2 for at least two years. If spouse #2 dies before you, you then collect 100% on his or her earnings. Nice work if you can get it.

As tempting as it may be, if you expect a long life, do not start collecting on your ex-spouse as soon as you turn 62. Each year of delay up to your full retirement age increases monthly benefits.

And whatever you do, never throw away old marriage licenses or divorce decrees, despite the probable strong urge. They may be needed when meeting with your social security administrator.

Strategies for Widows and Widowers

First, widows of any age may receive benefits if caring for the deceased spouse's child under age 16. The *child* of a deceased may also receive benefits while under age 18 (or up to age 19 if still full-time student in elementary or secondary school) Check with your social security office if you find yourself in this unique but unfortunate category.

Second, if married more than two years, at retirement age, the surviving spouse steps into the greater of their own or their spouse's benefits—if not remarried before age 60. If you happen to remarry before age 60, you lose the ability to use the benefits of your deceased spouse. *Therefore*: If you are entitled to wonderful survivor benefits from your late spouse, consider delaying marriage with the new honey until at least age 60!

A widow or widower, still single, may also begin receiving survivor's benefits at age 60, but I usually don't recommend it. You will receive 12% less than if you begin at age 62, and almost 30% less than if you waited until your full retirement age, usually between 66 and 67. As stated at the beginning of this chapter, review your health, work income potential, and life expectancy.

Every person widowed before retirement age and still single, or remarried after age 60, must find out from the Social Security Administration the eligible benefits they may be entitled to from their deceased spouse or ex-spouse. Always have a copy of the death certificate and marriage license in your files. Such information opens up several interesting strategies to maximize benefits.

Example: If my *lower*-income spouse died before I turned 60, I could start receiving their survivor's benefits when I am age 60, then switch over to my own higher benefits as early as 62. Essentially, I get two years free benefits. And the longer I choose to delay taking my own benefits while receiving the survivor benefits, my own monthly benefit amount will increase.

On the other hand, if I made *less* than my deceased spouse, that is, his or her benefits would be higher than mine, I can elect to take my own benefits starting at age 62 and delay taking my deceased spouse survivor benefits so that they grow to a higher monthly income amount. (Monthly benefits will continue to grow to what my spouse would have received at their full retirement age, so there is no benefit to delay taking them past my own full retirement age.) To recap, I take my lower benefit between ages 62 and, say 66½, then step into my higher deceased spouse benefits for the rest of my life.

From the two examples above, we see that the surviving spouse may choose which of the benefits—their own or their deceased spouse's—they can take sooner, and which they can take later and therefore allow to grow to a larger monthly amount.

Separately, if you or someone in the family of a deceased is disabled, check for benefit rules that apply to these situations.

Three Critical Takeaways from Chapter

1. The Social Security Administration pays lots of different benefits, not just to the worker who earned them. Be aware of spousal benefits, child benefits, disability benefits, divorced and survivor benefits.
2. With social security benefits, sometimes it pays to marry, sometimes it does not.
3. Realistically evaluate your life expectancy. If you greatly underestimate—or overestimate—its length, you could be short-changing yourself.

Chapter 16

Estate Planning: *I'll be Dead—Why Care?*

Three Great Myths

1. Probate is bad.
2. My will and trust control how my assets will be distributed at death.
3. My children—and my spouse's children—will all get along after I die.

For most of us, estate planning is all about controlling our assets to determine where they end up after we're gone. Estate planning should also encompass controlling our assets while we're alive if we are not able to control them ourselves because of incompetence or illness.

First, we must understand that just about everything in estate planning revolves around how we title our assets—in other words, the way in which we classify the ownership of our property, whether it's a mansion in Beverly Hills, or one share of Apple common stock.

Let's look at the three asset buckets below. No matter who we are, all our assets fall into these buckets, and these buckets determine what happens to our money and property if we lose our life—or lose our mind. The three buckets are: direct beneficiary assets, trust assets, and probate assets. That which you put in each of these buckets determines how your assets will pass on to others. Each bucket is independent of another.

Bucket #1	Bucket #2	Bucket #3
Assets Directly passed down to heirs: - Insurance Policies - IRAs - Joint assets - Transfer on Death Accounts - Annuities	Trust Assets - *Your* rules - No probate - Outright Distribution or held in trust longer	Probate/Will Assets - Everything not in Buckets 1, 2 - Normally outright distribution - Lawyers, delays

Bucket #1: Assets Directly Passed Down

First, let's look at direct beneficiary assets. Most of us have had assets in this bucket. As the chart indicates, it includes things like joint accounts, IRA accounts, life insurance policies, annuities, and pay-on-death accounts—also called Transfer-On-Death or TOD accounts.

For direct beneficiary assets, administration of the transfer to heirs is very straight forward. Such money or property titled this way goes directly to whom you name as a beneficiary or with whom you share a joint account. These funds do not go through your will or through a trust. When you die, the other person(s) named on the account grabs your death certificate and hands it into the financial institution and voilà, they become the new owner in receipt of your property.

Many clients believe that a will or a trust overrides money in a joint account or IRA. It does not. So, if your will shows that your wife gets all your money but the beneficiary to your IRA is your ex-wife, your wife cannot step in and receive the IRA. It goes to your ex.

Typically, if all of your assets are of a direct beneficiary nature then you may not need a will nor will you probably need a trust. For instance, if the only asset you have in the world is a joint account with your mother, you probably don't need a will or a trust. The will and trust buckets will be empty. When you die your mother becomes full owner of your joint account.

Note that there are two types of joint accounts. One, called *joint tenants with right of survivorship*, is one in which upon the death of one owner, the other joint holder becomes the sole owner of the entire account or asset. The second type of joint account, called *tenants in common ownership*, is one in which when one of the joint owners dies the other joint owner does not necessarily step into full ownership. The joint owner who died can pass their share to another person who potentially becomes a new joint owner of the asset.

As indicated before, when you have a direct beneficiary, including joint accounts, it overrides any other planning document like a will or a trust. So, if you have three children and a joint account with just one of them, after you die, there is no legal obligation for the child named on the joint account to share that money with their siblings. She has every legal right to keep 100% of the account or asset. After the parent dies, I have often witnessed this sibling explain to their brothers and sisters that mom wanted her to have 100% of the account because of all the help she gave to the parent. It is not usually a happy ending for the brothers and sisters.

For all direct beneficiary assets, including life insurance policies, the necessary task is to identify who the beneficiary is. If the beneficiary is not identified because the owner (decedent) did not properly complete a form, or the original beneficiary has died, then the asset may not go to *any* directed person, but instead, be dumped into the probate bucket. So, remember, every few years you should review your IRAs and life insurance policies to be sure that they list the up-to-date desired beneficiary.

Direct beneficiary assets that we've been discussing seem great because they are easy to understand, and they avoid the complexities of a trust or probate. But they are not appropriate in many situations, particularly those where there are complex family situations or major personality issues that could interfere with the proper management of money by the one inheriting. That is, when the direct beneficiary receives his money, he can do anything he wants with it, including blowing it on a wild weekend in Las Vegas.

Bucket #2: Trust Assets

Many clients ask if they need a trust. After advising them to seek advice from an attorney, I ask them if they know what a trust is. Most of us really don't and are confused by the myths surrounding trusts. I make specific recommendations for whether you need a trust later within the section "Basic Estate Strategies for Various Life Stages".

In simplest terms, a trust is a bucket in which we put assets. The way we put assets into the trust is to change the name or change the title of the asset to the name of the trust. Once in the bucket, these trust assets must follow the rules that we establish for the trust. In short, a trust is a bucket of assets with instructions set out as to what to do with the assets. If the trust has lots of instructions but no assets titled in the trust, then the trust has no power or influence over anything. Further, if the trust has lots of assets titled in its name but the instructions are lousy, then the trust is lousy. For you to have a good trust, you must have the appropriate assets titled in the trust and a good set of instructions of what to do with the assets.

Let's talk about another confusing area, the parties to a trust. There are several, and often, each of these can be the same person.

The grantor, sometimes called the settlor, establishes the trust and puts assets in it. This is the person who creates the instructions of the trust and retitles specific assets to be in the trust bucket, a process called funding the trust. The grantor is usually the one who can change the instructions of the trust, too.

The trustee is the manager of the trust, responsible for carrying out the instructions and administration of the trust. Typically, the grantor—again, the person who starts the trust—is the initial trustee, too. If the first trustee gets sick or dies, then there is usually a successor trustee, as indicated in the trust instructions.

The beneficiary is the person(s) named within the instructions of the trust to receive assets, and/or income—at some point—either currently or at the time of death of someone (usually the grantor or spouse), in the future. The grantor can also be the beneficiary and usually is so while alive, most commonly in a revocable trust. A non-person, such as a charity or pet, (through an appointed caregiver) can also be a beneficiary.

In short, the person setting up the trust can initially be all three parties, the grantor, trustee, and beneficiary.

Revocable and Irrevocable Trusts

Since I mentioned revocable trust, let's briefly explain the difference between that and a trust that is irrevocable.

As the names imply, a *revocable* trust can be changed, but typically only by the grantor-originators. This is very handy because, during a lifetime, the grantor will often want to put new assets in or remove assets from the trust, change beneficiaries, or revise other instructions, such as including a new grandchild as a beneficiary, or excluding the family drug addict.

For tax purposes, the IRS views a revocable trust as one and the same with the grantor-originator person(s), as long as the grantor is also the trustee-manager. Therefore, all income and tax reporting go conveniently on the grantor's normal 1040 tax form.

Note well: A revocable trust usually provides no tax advantage, nor does it protect against creditors' claims or lawsuits. This misconception is widespread. You need an irrevocable trust to do these things, but for a price: the loss of control.

An *irrevocable* trust is much more *inflexible* than one established as revocable. When the grantor transfers—that is, retitles—assets into an irrevocable trust bucket, the assets are essentially given away. You the grantor, can only get access to the assets or their income on a limited basis or not at all, subject to rules that you have initially designed, but will have difficulty changing. That is why most trusts are not designed to be initially irrevocable.

For instance, I may not want creditors or claimants to get to my assets, so I put them in an irrevocable trust. As a result, the people who sue me in the future can't get to the assets, but maybe I can't either, very easily. Let's say I have a change of heart and want to withdraw a big chunk of funds to donate to my church. If I forgot to include that provision in the trust instructions, I cannot legally do it. Indeed, I may have to go to court and have a judge approve my desire to amend terms of my own irrevocable trust.

Putting (retitling) money or property into an irrevocable trust is equivalent to gifting your assets away. Those assets become no longer yours, and if they generate income, the trust, viewed as a separate legal entity, may have to file its own tax return and pay income tax.

The trick with an irrevocable trust is to set provisions—that is instructions—flexible enough so that if you want to get to the assets or enjoy the income, you can, but still have the protection so that these same assets are considered legally *sheltered* from other parties, such as, plaintiffs, business associates, and future ex-spouses.

It's interesting to note that once a grantor-originator of a *revocable* trust dies or becomes legally incompetent, the trust converts to an irrevocable trust. Why? Because the only party who can revoke or change the trust is no longer able to do so. As a result, provisions in the trust cannot be altered, including terms for beneficiaries receiving assets. And new assets cannot be placed in the trust nor removed unless existing rules in the trust allow for such transfers.

Bucket #3: Probate (Will) Assets

Those assets that don't fall into the first two buckets—either the direct beneficiary bucket or trust bucket—end up in the third bucket. This is the residual bucket and it is only these assets over which instructions in a person's *will* will have any control. Yes, if someone tells you they've named you in their will, but all their assets are in joint accounts or a trust, don't book that Hawaiian cruise just yet; there may be no assets left for you.

Indeed, many people are so organized with trusts and direct beneficiary accounts, they have very few assets remaining for a will to direct. Residual assets may just include furniture, an auto, and a minor checking account.

And unlike a trust, which can help the originator control assets while still living, the instructions of a will only kick in after the will maker, called the testator (sometimes testatrix for a female), dies.

Probate: Unlike a trust, which is a private document that does not go through the public court system, a will is reviewed by a judge and may be viewed by the general public. This is not always bad, but may not always be desired by the family. Our system is set up so that when someone makes a will and instructs the distribution of assets subject to the will, it is reviewed by our judicial system, in effect, a judge. His or her oversight function includes making sure a) the person appointed in the instructions of the will to administer it is appropriate, b) the will is valid, and c) that the instructions of distribution in the will are faithfully executed by the appointed representative. The appointed representative is called an executor or, in some states, a personal representative.

This process of judicial review and administration is called probate. It often has a bad connotation of delays and expense, but in many estate administrations we are lucky to have it. Several situations arise in which there are family controversies, or the competency and ability of the testator to execute their will comes into question. In these cases, family members and other interested parties welcome such oversight by a legal authority.

What happens to assets in this probate bucket if there is no properly executed will—or no will at all? Then rules of the State determine how such assets are divided among heirs. For instance, in Florida, state law says that if a spouse dies intestate (without a will), his or her surviving spouse *does not* automatically get 100% of the assets that could have been willed (Bucket #3 assets only) to the spouse. Instead, the surviving spouse gets only half of those assets if the deceased had children with one or more earlier mates.

The rules of each state may vary, and without a will, there could be lots of surprises for the heirs, especially in this period of multiple marriages and children of unmarried parents. A will is more important than ever. Just ask the family members of rock star Prince who died without a properly executed will and caused havoc for family members.

Basic Estate Strategies for Various Life Stages

Now let's take a few minutes to review guidelines that we should consider for our estate planning tasks as we move through various stages of life. Most of us struggle with trying to figure out if we need a will or a trust or that mysterious doodad they call a durable power of attorney. Your particular situation may require special attention, but I've broken the categories into five stages of life:

1. Young single person
2. Young couple
3. Couple in their 40's
4. Older married couple
5. Older single person

1. Young single person - If there are few assets, which is typical, you may not even need a will, let alone a trust. If you die, the few assets that you have will go back to your parents. Your 401(k) account is a Bucket #1 asset whereby you can directly assign the beneficiary(ies), such as a parent or your love mate.

If there are significant assets, you should probably have a will and possibly a revocable trust. The revocable trust is important because it allows you to control assets before, as well as after, death. If issues appear to be complex, see an attorney who deals with estate planning issues.

Even if you have few assets, but you have an unstable family situation, such as a parent who is incarcerated or who cannot manage money properly, a will or a trust may be the only way you're going to keep assets away from the troubled family member. Again, in most states, single people without children will have their assets go to their parents if there is no will or trust directing otherwise. As I'll repeat in this section, for difficult situations and creative solutions, seek the help of an estate planning attorney.

2. Young couple - The typical young couple just starting out may also have few assets. If married, most of their assets will be jointly owned and each person will normally be a beneficiary of the other's IRA or 401(k) account. In most cases, if there's no will, it's not a disaster.

However, these days many couples are not married. In this situation, I highly recommend a will. And, if assets are significant or there are troubling family situations, I suggest you investigate establishing a revocable trust, too.

For unmarried couples, I usually recommend titling assets separately. IRA and pension accounts are, by definition, separate. Separately owned assets, even for married couples who end up legally divorcing and splitting marital assets, may allow easier division, and often allow couples to focus on their individual financial goals. By the way, if one of the partners in an unmarried relationship stubbornly insists on joint ownership, be careful of ulterior relationship motives.

If a couple has managed to somehow title all their assets jointly, then a will or trust will have no authority over the assets. That is, if one dies, the other partner will step into sole ownership if assets are titled joint with right of survivorship.

3. Couple in their 40s - By this stage of life there may be children and some accumulation of assets, such as a home and 401(k) accounts. Notwithstanding my usual recommendation of separating assets, most assets will probably be categorized as Box #1 assets, such as, jointly owned assets and direct beneficiary life insurance policies. Box #1 assets bypass a will or trust.

A will, however, is recommended if there are assets not jointly owned. For instance, a will should be made if a parent has assets individually owned and wishes they go to a child from a prior relationship, or, if one of the parties in the couple owns an interest in a business or privately held corporation.

A trust should be considered if there are assets outside joint accounts that are to go to minor children from a prior relationship. A trust should also be considered if family complications exist, such as a disability, an addiction problem, or a money management issue.

4. Older married couple - By this time, the couple's children have usually left the nest—we hope!—and retirement is here or close at hand. There are more assets now and fewer mortgages. But like the younger couple, especially those married, many assets will be jointly owned. In an idyllic family, where everyone gets along and is financially stable, a will is recommended, and perhaps a trust may not be essential. The thinking is that when one of the partners gets sick or dies, the other partner will be there to step in, manage affairs, and eventually inherit what's left, eliminating the need for a trust.

Unfortunately for most of us, but fortunately for attorneys and financial planners, we don't have idyllic families, but a web of complications, such as second and third marriages, stepchildren floating around, and a good dose of general unpredictability. A trust (one for each partner if not legally married) is best to accommodate the needs of more complex circumstances.

Legacy trust: For those couples who have more than $200,000 in assets and who plan to leave most of their money to children or other close relatives, I and many attorneys recommend what is commonly called a legacy trust. A legacy trust starts out as a revocable trust, but it includes provisions that your heirs will *not* receive their inherited money outright when you die. Instead, after you're gone, the money will stay in the trust and be distributed to the heirs over time based on formulas and instructions you design. Yes, your heirs may complain about the idea of not receiving the right to use all of their inheritance immediately after you die, but a legacy trust is there for their protection. By keeping your money in trust for them after you're gone, the money is protected from: their claimants, their potential irresponsibility in managing money, and their future ex-spouses. Provisions normally allow for them to receive regular income and even special distributions if pre-defined needs arise. In a well-designed trust, the beneficiary heir can actually have her cake and eat it, too.

In the past, only Rockefellers and Kennedys used this estate planning technique; now estate planners recommend a legacy trust for virtually everybody, because, as we get older, it doesn't take much to accumulate $200,000. Many people think it clever to title assets jointly, or place money in a Transfer-on-death account in order to avoid probate or the need for a trust. But they may be short-changing their heirs and future generations of the family because such direct beneficiary accounts (Bucket #1) may easily be passed down to heirs, only to be dissipated along the way.

Google it or check with your attorney to learn more. Note that like other revocable trusts you create, after you are dead the trust becomes irrevocable, meaning it is difficult to change or amend. For your situation, this could be very important. These few paragraphs could well be the most important of this entire book. Just ask the Rockefellers who have managed to pass millions down to several generations of family.

5. Older single person - This is the divorcee, widow, or older bachelor who may not have a significant "other" in his life right now. They are retired, or getting close to retirement, and have accumulated perhaps significant assets. It should almost go without saying that these persons need a will. When they die, the world needs to know how their assets are to be distributed. It is not fair to friends or relatives handling post-life affairs for them to step into an unorganized mess of paperwork and accounts.

Even more than a married couple, the single person will need a trust if they have significant assets, say more than $200,000, in

Bucket #3—that is, assets that would normally go through probate. Again, a trust not only helps manage assets after the person has died, but also helps manage assets while the person is still living. Establishing provisions that relate to caring for a person are becoming more and more important as our lives linger through assisted living facilities and nursing homes. Without the trust, a substitute caregiver may have to go through the court system to get a judge's permission to be guardian. This can be a time-consuming and expensive mess.

If your assets are less than $200,000 and you have responsible children—and they get along with each other—then having assets titled as much as possible in Bucket #1, such as joint or Transfer-on-Death accounts, should be OK without needing a trust. But remember, if you have an asset owned jointly with your child, this asset becomes potentially subject to claims against *them* in *their* lawsuits and divorces.
(I feel obligated to mention this, but I've never seen it happen in 30 years of practice. Be advised at your own risk and seek legal advice.)

Three Documents Everyone Needs

In addition to a trust or will, which may not be needed for every adult, the need for the following documents has no exception, save perhaps for those already deemed legally incompetent to create their own authorized instruments. Otherwise, if you're past the age of 17 and you have a heartbeat, you need these three.

1. *A durable power of attorney*: This document outlines the legal authority you give to another person to act on your behalf <u>while you are living.</u> The word durable indicates you do not have to be disabled or legally incompetent for this other person to act in your stead. This document is necessary because we never know when we could have that serious auto accident or debilitating stroke. You need to tell the world who has your authority to pay bills, to perform bank transactions, manage your real estate, or register an automobile.
2. *Health care surrogate*: This document assigns someone to represent you to healthcare givers if you can't do it yourself. As a surrogate myself for others, medical professionals and hospitals have relied on my input to authorize medicines,

surgical procedures, and even medical transportation for patients who were not able to make these decisions themselves. Often, healthcare surrogate authority is included within the durable power of attorney document.

3. *A living will*: Having advance healthcare directives, such as a living will in place, can help prevent prolonged, painful, expensive, and emotionally burdensome issues from arising during end-of-life treatment. A living will directs how you want to be treated in certain situations, such as if you are terminally ill, mentally incapacitated, or suffering from life-threatening injuries. You may wish to have as much medical intervention as possible, or you may decide to forgo certain types of life-sustaining treatment, such as ventilators or heart-lung machines. You create this document not only for yourself, but out of consideration of those who will be caring for you. Believe it or not, researchers have found that attending medical professionals often misinterpret or do not fully read the document. Review your wishes with your healthcare surrogate at the time of drafting the living will so they know your intentions beforehand.

The Issue of Legal Competency

When I talk to attorneys about the determination of establishing competency in a person who is creating or amending a legal estate document, they often respond with an expression akin to admitting that during childhood they once stole their neighbor's bicycle. It is an uncomfortable conversation. And it's uncomfortable because competency can be variable from one day to the next and dependent upon the judgment of the people in the room with the person signing the documents. In short, legal competency is often in the eye of the beholder.

The issue of incompetency is not just dealing with grandpa who is in early or late stage dementia. It is the elderly aunt who feebly succumbs to the pushy niece to change her will. It is the elderly widower bewitched and bedazzled by the younger female caregiver into leaving her the house. I have seen elderly people completely coherent in the morning, then four hours later, be in a hopeless fog.

Are they legally competent? One attorney told me they were in the morning; then they were *not* in the afternoon.

In Florida, the courts have ruled that someone who could be incompetent can, at times, have a "lucid interval," giving them legal capacity to execute legal documents. With this grayness in the law, good luck to the family member arguing to the judge that Uncle Harry was incompetent when he gave his house to the sexy home caregiver. The burden of proof is on the nephew to show that his uncle was *not* of legal capacity at that particular time.

Legal competency of course becomes an issue when heirs dispute what they believe to be the *true* intentions of the deceased. Circumstances, witnesses, and hard evidence then come into play, often end up in the courtroom, and may eat up substantial assets.

If you are involved as either the one signing estate plans or the person assisting a relative or friend, be aware that what you design and sign could be later questioned for its validity due to legal incompetency. Have witnesses around you that can vouch for the fact that documents were created and signed with clarity and reason.

The best advice is usually to include a lawyer in the process. The good attorneys will often ask friends and relatives accompanying mom to momentarily step out of the office. Then, in private consult with the lawyer, mom can confide without visible influence what her wishes are. Such a conference also allows the attorney to assess the mental state of her client more accurately, and provide confidence that when the documents are signed, there is no coercion or confusion.

Do I Really Need a Lawyer to do Estate Planning?

The foregoing paragraph leads us to the answer: Yes!

I know you can get templates for virtually all the documents we discuss in this chapter from Google searches. So, do we really need a lawyer who may just print out the same forms? Maybe not if you have the simplest life in the world and perhaps hate everyone equally. But it's worth it to pay someone several hundred dollars or even a few thousand to make sure your many thousands go to the right places and people.

Plus, once you establish a relationship with an attorney, you have someone you know to call for legal advice if something comes up in your life, and not just about wills and trusts. Things may come up like auto accidents, marital issues, child support, and how to sue your neighbor when her nutty son crashes into your fence with his Harley. Me, I have an attorney for estate planning, another for real estate, another for divorces (ouch!), one for business deals, and yes, one more to play golf with—in case somebody hits me with a ball.

Three Critical Takeaways from Chapter

1. Some documents, such as wills and trusts, may only be needed in certain circumstances, but there are other legal documents, such as a durable power of attorney, that virtually everyone should have.
2. We live in a complicated world. Be prepared for legal complexity.
3. Seeking the advice and experience of a good estate attorney is probably the best money you can spend in estate planning.

Chapter 17

Gifting Your Money to Others: Finally Explained

Three Great Myths

1. Annual gifts to others should be limited to $15,000 per person to avoid taxes.
2. The person who receives a gift from another person must pay income tax on that gift.
3. The person who gives the gift must often pay taxes.

The idea of how much we can gift to another person without tax consequences should be, at first glance, the easiest thing to get our arms around, but it is easily the most misunderstood concept that crosses my path. Even at cocktail parties, with well-off retirees, there is confusion. And stubborn confusion. When a well-off senior tells me that my explanation is wrong, I smugly offer credentials that I'm a registered investment advisor, a CPA, have created and managed a four-office advisory firm, and earned an MBA from a top school that included lots of tax courses. They still insist I'm wrong!

Here is the one sentence headline: **Unless you gift away to other people during your lifetime a total that exceeds $13.61 million, neither you nor the gift receiver pays *any* tax. Zero, zilch, nada.**

Realize that when we dare talk about *having* $13.61 million over a lifetime to even give away, this narrows the potential group of people down to less than half a percent of the US population. Therefore, the other 99.5% of the population—that's virtually all of us—never have to worry about reaching this limit—and therefore never pay taxes on gifts given or received.

Note that a gift to a person is not the same as a charitable contribution. Giving your kids $5,000 or letting them have the family sofa when they move out is not charity for tax deduction purposes. Charitable deductions are reserved for donations you give to official charities, such as religious organizations or 501(c)3 organizations like The American Cancer Society. Charitable donations have an entirely different set of rules from those of personal gifts we discuss in this chapter.

Most people who mention the $18,000 annual gift limit believe that if the gift to another person exceeds this amount, somebody somewhere will be stuck paying some tax. Wrong!

The IRS and Congress add confusion to this issue by increasing the annual amount that we all talk about. Many years ago the $18,000 used to be $10,000, but has gradually risen over the years, indexed for inflation. For a few years, the amount was $15,000, but by 2024 the figure had risen to $18,000. However, even after all this time many clients still ask me, "So, how does that $10,000 gift rule work?"

Under current rules, for 99.5% of us, if we gift to someone more than $18,000 within a given year, the only ramification is that we must file what I describe as an information form with the IRS. That's it. There is no tax due. There are no negative effects for the gift receiver nor does he have to file any form or return with the IRS. The information form which the gift giver must file is IRS Form 709. But, generally no tax will be due with this form.

The background for this $18,000 information report, Form 709, requires some explaining, but if you don't care about the logic and just need to know the mechanics, you can skip the following five paragraphs and move down to where I provide additional gifting tips.

The logic of these gift rules is actually part of our federal estate tax rules, also known in the vernacular as the death tax. Unlike normal income taxes most of us pay on earnings and investment *income*, the estate tax is imposed on the *asset values* we own at time of death, something akin to property taxes. But in addition to real estate assets, we must include all property we own, such as money, investments, and even life insurance policies that pay out once we kick the bucket. If you're not familiar with this federal asset tax, it's probably because one does not have to pay it unless assets exceed $13.61 million. That's right, it is a tax on dead rich people. If we die with assets over $13.61 million, the tax on the excess is a whopping 40% on the excess. To put it another way, if you are worth $1 billion on your deathbed, the minute you sign out of here for the great beyond, your estate essentially drops by 40%, or about $544 million, the approximate amount of estate tax due Uncle Sam.

Now here is where the $18,000 annual gift thing comes in that everyone talks about. The IRS is not stupid. They know that we're not stupid either and that if we think we're going to be taxed at 40% on excess assets, right before we turn the oxygen machine off, we're going to escape the estate tax by gifting our assets away to relatives and others, by at least the necessary amount to get our total estate below the $13.61 million exemption amount.

To prevent these deathbed giveaways from reducing our estate in order to avoid the estate tax, the IRS—actually Congress—has created a rule that says any gifts you give away—*during your entire life*—will be mathematically <u>added back to your estate</u> total to figure if your assets exceed the $13.61 million. So, Bill Gates can forget about those deathbed gifts to his BFFs.

I'm getting to the $18,000, right now. Out of the kindness of their heart, the IRS has an exception to the "add all your lifetime gifts back to your estate" rule: They allow us to gift up to $18,000 per year per person without adding those gifts back to our estate upon death. I suppose it is their way of permitting millionaires to let something slip out of the estate during their lifetimes.

Because the IRS does not know if we are a millionaire or not, however, they require everyone who gives a gift to someone within a given year that exceeds $18,000 to file an information report (Form 709) to keep the IRS informed of these excess gifts. In that way, upon your death the IRS can add up all the lifetime excess gifts, combine them with what you own at time of death, to determine if they exceed $13.61 million. If they do, then your estate pays an estate tax. For the 99.5% of us that will not have assets this great, there will never be a tax, so neither we—nor the gift receiver—ever have to worry about the amount of gifts to others.

If all that still doesn't clarify the annual $18,000 gift limit rule, don't worry. Just know that unless you are a multi multi-millionaire, there is no tax to pay on gifts given to others.

Some Clarification and Tips about Gifting to Others

Charities: A gift to a charity such as a church or the Red Cross is not the same as a gift to another person or to a person who is not a qualified charity. There are different rules for each. In fact, if you gift your money to a charity either during your life or as a post-death provision in your trust or will, these amounts are not added back to your estate for calculating estate taxes. As a result, somebody like Warren Buffett, who is worth $80 billion but promises to leave 75 billion of it to charity, has just reduced his taxable estate down to $5 billion. The estate tax on $5 billion is approximately $2 billion. If, on the other hand, he would simply leave his $80 billion to family and friends, the estate tax would be approximately 40% of $80 billion or $32 billion. Yes, Uncle Sam has lost out big-time on the Buffett estate, but so has his family, if you call inheriting $5 billion missing out.

Spouses: Gifts to legally married spouses do not have to be counted as gifts, either for the $18,000 annual reporting or for assets inherited.

Medical: Qualified Medical expenses that a person pays for a friend or relative are not counted as gifts when calculating the $18,000 per year issue or when adding back assets at the end of life. So, if you happen to pay for your grandchild's braces that cost $10,000 and additionally give him $10,000 cash for a trip to Europe, the total gift that counts is only the $10,000 cash. Since $10,000 is less than $18,000, it does not have to be added back into the estate at death nor is there any annual Form 709 gift reporting required.

Education: This one is similar to the medical expense exception above. If you pay for someone's higher education, it does not count as a gift. Note, however, that, like medical expenses, the payment must be made directly to the institution, not to the relative who then pays the tuition or medical expense.

As stated, if you gift more than $18,000 to a person within the same calendar year, other than the exceptions just described, you must file IRS Form 709 to let the IRS know. To potentially avoid filing this form, consider splitting the gifts among several people. That is, if you plan to give, say, $20,000 to a married son, give him $10,000 and his wife $10,000. Or, if you're married, you and your spouse could each give a gift, and if giving to a married couple, you could give a total of up to $72,000 in a year without filing Form 709 by each of you giving $18,000 to each of them.

Finally, if you spread gifts over multiple calendar years, you'll be able to give larger amounts without having to file Form 709.

Again, even if you exceed the $18,000 gift amount in a year, no tax is due unless taxable gifts over your life exceed $13.61 million. So, relax!

Now, at cocktail parties, you can be the smartest one when discussing gift taxes. But they probably won't believe you, either.

Three Critical Takeaways from Chapter

1. For 99.5% of us, we can give and receive financial gifts without any tax liability arising.
2. If a person gifts to someone more than $18,000 within a calendar year, IRS Form 709 should be filed, but for 99.5% of us, no tax will be due with it.
3. There are several ways to stay under the $18,000 reporting amount, including allocating gifts among recipients and calendar years.

Chapter 18

Nursing Home and Long-Term Care Planning Summed Up: Die Fast

Three Great Myths

1. Most of us end up in a nursing home—and for a long time.
2. Most of us won't make it to 90, so why worry about it?
3. We'll be able to be cared for in our own home when we need help because we have enough money to pay for such care.

It may be surprising, but this, more than all other chapters, should be read by every generation, because planning for the care of the elderly involves and affects everyone.

Elder care is also one area that no one wants to discuss, even less so than death itself.

Planning for the care of the elderly, including yourself eventually, usually involves a lot of wishful thinking and hoping. We hope that we can die quickly enough to avoid the need for nursing care, we hope mom has enough money saved to receive the care at home she wants, or we hope that, somehow, dad can move in with us toward the end of his life for a smooth finish. Too often, the realities of getting old and dying make this phase of life anything but smooth. Personalities, geographic distances, illness, family relationships, and financial constraints create the unexpected—and all its accompanying stress.

Most of us hope that we and our relatives will not have to go through the slow process of decline in our later years in which outside help or other extended care by others is required. We would love to live to at least a ripe old age of 90 with some aches and pains and limitations, but generally have our mind and abilities intact. Then, when all of our other friends and relatives have already left this earth and a desire to continue living has waned, we can have a quick and sudden heart attack on the tennis court—or cruise ship—and be out of here. Even if we can't hope for that, maybe we can hope for a disease that rapidly kills us.

These kinds of quick deaths are frequent, and statistically, happen for about 30 percent of those dying. The rest of us may or may not be so lucky.

What actually are the odds that a person 65 years or older will need long-term care assistance?

About 70%, or 7 in ten of us.

What are the odds that a person 65 years or older will need actual nursing home assistance?

About 35%, or almost 4 in ten of us.

The average time in a nursing home is 2½ years—a little longer for women, a little shorter for men.

That only 30% of seniors will *not* need long-term care assistance is understandable as healthcare providers make improvements in treating things that formerly killed us quickly, such as heart attacks and, to a lesser degree, cancer. Notwithstanding these advances, old bodies still weaken and eventually reveal other chronic illnesses, such as dementia and severe arthritis.

Evolution of the Retiree—in Three Major Phases

Returning to the 70% of seniors that *will* need long term care assistance, let's look at some typical paths as they travel from active retirees to dependent nursing home patients.

<u>Retiree Phase I—Young and Active, Age 60 to 75</u>

1. After retiring from a job, the retiree often moves to a retirement community, such as those in Florida or Arizona, leaving close relatives and friends in other states behind, while perhaps making short annual return visits.
2. The retiree lives successfully, usually with a life partner, enjoying leisure activities and travel.

3. The partners are both highly functional, supporting each other socially, financially, and physically.
4. When the first partner eventually gets ill, the second partner becomes the caretaker of the other, helping to prolong his or her life. Unfortunately, the caretaker may decline during this period, too, due to additional physical and emotional stress.

Retiree Phase II—Slowing Down, Age 75 to 83

1. When the first partner dies, the second partner usually stays in the current retirement community, but a little more socially isolated because they participate in couples activities less.
2. As the surviving senior ages, she increasingly drops out of social circles and reduces physical exercise.
3. If a hospital stay is required, the senior does well at this stage, easily supported by a close friend or a visiting relative, usually an adult child. The hospital stay is short and treatment well defined.
4. As time goes on, the senior, unless he or she has remarried, strives to stay engaged in organizations and recreation that keeps them active outside the home. Things like family, church, golf, bridge clubs, and travel groups, usually are important parts of the daily schedule. Doctor visits—typically done alone now—become another important part of the day.
5. Eventually, age begins to catch up with our active senior. He stays home more, several of his friends have died or moved away, and he is determined to remain living in the same house and community in which he has lived now going on possibly 20 years or more.

Retiree Phase III—Nearing End of Life, Beyond Age 83

1. The weakness and fragility of old age leave the senior with less physical activity, a poorer diet, and growing isolation. Early dementia may be evident, but everyone around her wants to deny it, especially the senior herself who wants to maintain

her independence in daily activities. Her children, who may live at a great distance, may also resist.

2. Hospital stays are more complicated now. The senior may have more intractable or chronic illnesses, and the support of an almost full-time healthcare advocate, such as a close friend or family member, is needed.
3. When the senior returns home from the hospital, weakened by age and illness, poor nutrition and isolation result in more difficulties, surprise falls, mysterious symptoms, and anxiety from relatives and friends who care about this person.
4. Discussion among family members begins about how to bring in extra care.
5. Inevitably, our senior falls again, or has a spell, or gets into an auto accident, and in a weakened state, enters the hospital once again.
6. After the hospital can do no more, the patient is sent to a rehabilitation center to re-strengthen and prepare for the return to home. Family and friends are consoled by this, with what has become for seniors, a typical, and perhaps recurring, path and plan of action. Our patient still intends to somehow live out her life in a home she retired to many years ago. Presumption: Home healthcare will be brought in if necessary and be financially feasible.
7. A home healthcare assistant is brought in, but more complications arise. The senior does not get along with her. Or the home healthcare person cannot be there all the hours needed. Or there are not enough funds to pay for such care, or the family chooses not to pay for such care.
8. Our senior may end up receiving assisted living services at this point. States may refer to this type of service as assisted living services, residential care, adult foster care, personal home care, or supported living. Most assisted living services occur at group facilities called—you guessed it—assisted living facilities or ALFs. To be under such care, the resident usually has difficulty doing one of the five activities of daily living

commonly listed: bathing, dressing, toileting, eating, and remembering to administer medications.

9. Rather than an ALF, the senior may move in with one of his children. However, the children soon realize that caring for a sick, elderly person requires time, expertise, and patience they may not have. There are not many children who have the fortitude to do intimate bathroom duties for their parents. I know I would not.
10. As a last resort, and it always is a last resort, the parent, the same once active senior who travelled the world and played golf with the best of them, ends up in a nursing home, also called a skilled nursing facility. He probably spends most of his time in a wheelchair, uses a walker if he's lucky, but may simply spend a great deal of the day in bed. And the worst part is, except for chronic pain, he may not remember the places he travelled to or the rounds of golf played.

If you think you're depressed reading through this progression, you may imagine how I felt writing it—especially because I remember that a similar path will occur for 70% of us. Fortunately for the seniors we describe here, their *early* retirement years were wonderful. Most retirees, unfortunately, will not even have the luxury of world travel or golf at the country club.

Financing Old Age Care

Let's take a breath—albeit a short one—to talk about financing this path of care.

Medicare

While Medicare covers most retiree medical costs to some degree, for nursing home stays, Medicare covers only the first 100 days, and with stipulations. Some of these Medicare requirements are:

1. The patient must first have a three-day in-patient hospital stay,
2. The ensuing treatment in the nursing home must be related to the hospital stay,

3. Nursing home admission must be no more than 30 days after the hospital stay, and
4. Only the first 20 days are fully covered; the remaining 80 days are covered up to only $176 per day. The remainder falls to the patient or to a supplemental Medicare insurance policy purchased earlier.

After the 100-day period, the cost of skilled nursing care, whether administered in a large nursing home, small care facility, or the patient's residence, is not covered by any *medical* insurance. This is the stark reality facing 70% of us.

Medicare pays for no assisted living care services except those that are directly medically related, such as medicines (under its Part D program), physical therapy, or other medical procedures.

Medicaid

For those with insufficient assets and income, Medicaid will kick in to pay for nursing home costs. Also, patients who are veterans may be fortunate to find a nursing home funded by the Veterans Administration, but there is often a long waiting list.

Medicaid is for those with few assets—that is, the poorer in our society. If you are a millionaire, you will probably not qualify to have Medicaid pay for your nursing home costs.

Medicaid rules vary by state, so you should check what's happening where you live.

Let's look at Florida to see what its limits are in 2019. To qualify for Medicaid to pay all your nursing home costs, your monthly income must be no more than $2,313. Double that if a married couple is pursuing Medicaid long term care assistance. For assets, the limit is a measly $2,000, or $3,000, excluding house and vehicle, for both spouses trying to qualify. If only one spouse needs nursing home care, the other spouse may keep a house valued up to $713,000, one car, and other assets up to $154,440.

Many clients ask about gifting their assets away, or executing other strategies, to make it appear they are poor enough to qualify for Medicaid assistance. On the surface, this makes sense because we fear that after we've spent our whole life scraping and saving in order to have a comfortable retirement and to pass much of our assets on to our children, most of what we have accumulated may be consumed during a very expensive stay in a nursing home.

Some of these strategies to qualify for Medicaid involve buying annuities, selling real estate, and retitling assets in the name of the children. But be careful. These gambits often come with gotchas of their own. For instance, the type of annuity required by Medicaid to make it look like the asset has disappeared is one in which no residual value exists for heirs after you're gone. But the annuity salesman will not tell you that. And if you sell or retitle real estate, you may be creating unnecessary capital gains taxes. Overshadowing all of this is a rule that most states have called the look-back rule, which says that even if you gift away your assets to qualify for Medicaid, the state is allowed to "look back" at these gifts and add them back to classify them as *your* assets if you've gifted them within the last five years (Florida).

For this area of planning, I cannot recommend enough that you seek professional planning. There are attorneys who specialize in helping you to structure your assets so that the risk of great loss is minimized. Such counsel is money well spent.

Medicaid and Assisted Care Services: Some states may fund various assisted living expenses, too, but many do not. Medicaid does not cover room and board for such services, but if the patient is receiving assisted care services, the facility must be Medicaid-certified, nonetheless.

If you happen to be receiving SSI (that is, Social Security's Supplemental Security Income program), you are already qualified for Medicaid support for nursing home costs in many states, including Florida.

Note: Not every nursing home accepts Medicaid Long Term Care payments. Some people will tell you that those which do not, that is, the facilities that accept only private pay or private insurance, are better quality, but I have not seen that as a blanket truth. However, many facilities know you may run out of money and thereby eventually qualify for Medicaid and lower rates; these companies do not want that. As a counter action, many retirement living organizations require a large deposit and even a review of your finances before they accept you for residency, even to their independent living section. This is particularly true if the organization is a transition facility, that is, one that has living units for their residents to transition over the years from independent living, to assisted living, and then nursing home care. By the time you transition to their nursing home unit, they hope you do not qualify for Medicaid, so you can continue to pay higher private-pay rates that exceed those paid by Medicaid.

Insurance

Having an insurance policy to cover potential nursing home costs is a good idea. Over the last several years, insurance companies thought the same and so did many of their customers. Unfortunately, insurance companies discovered they underestimated claim costs, the rate of utilization by its insured customers, and how long they lived once they entered the nursing home. As a result, new policies to cover nursing home costs, called long term care policies, have been restructured and are, for the most part, unaffordable to purchase.

As a result, the only exception when it may make sense to buy one of these conventional long-term care policies is if you know you have a very high likelihood of needing a nursing home, and will probably live in one for many years. Add to this the supposition that you have significant assets, say more than $500,000, to protect. The best example of this: Through some special knowledge of family history or gene testing, you, the patient, know you eventually will suffer from dementia.

An alternative that is growing in popularity to the conventional long-term care policy is to buy a hybrid life insurance policy that includes a feature to use death benefits *before* you die for nursing home care. The insurance company basically says that if you buy their policy, they'll give you a choice how to use the death benefits: either a payout upon death, or alternatively, assistance to pay for the cost of nursing home care.

Here is an example of features of a real policy I recently viewed:

- Premium Payment: One-time cost of $100,000.
- Insurance company promises to pay in long-term care benefits: $450,000.

- Insurance company promises to pay at death if no long-term care benefits are needed: $150,000.
- After five years, and no death or benefits used, customers can choose to get the $100,000 premium refunded.

The policy was quoted for a healthy 60-year old. You can actually see the odds the insurance company is placing on the need and cost of long-term care and estimated years of life expectancy. Their actuaries are willing to be on the hook for $450,000 of nursing care, say, 25 years from now in return for having $100,000 of your money in their pockets now. In the meantime, their profit comes from investing that $100,000 during the same expected 25 years.

<u>Self-Pay</u>

If you do not qualify for Medicaid, and you do not have insurance, I will venture to guess that the cost of care will come out of your own pocket, typically termed self- or private-pay. The bad news is that, as I've said, there is a 70% chance that you will need long-term care. The good news is that the average time is 2½ years. Depending on the location and quality of your chosen care facility—those in the south are less expensive than those in the north and west—this length of time should not break the bank—if the bank has a healthy balance. Assuming that the monthly cost of nursing care is typically between $5,000 and $9,000, let's use $100,000 as a projected annual cost. At 2½ years, that is a total out-of-pocket cost of $250,000. And, the 30% of seniors who statistically will not enter a nursing home will not spend any of this.

My personal experience working with clients and family over the years has borne out the survey averages. However, I also see a trend of longer times in nursing homes due to advancement in physical medicine and the higher likelihood of lingering diseases related to dementia that allow the older person to linger longer.

<u>Small Care Nursing Facility</u>

Also called an adult family care home. In Florida, the operator of such a facility must live there. Patient occupancy is limited to five. As a category, these places fall into the assisted living category, but I have seen most of them actually doing the yeoman's work of a nursing home. Licensing by state authorities is stringent. Medicaid and other agencies recognize such facilities for cost sharing.

For the family who feels uncomfortable with the size and institutionalism of a large nursing facility, check out this alternative. Costs are usually lower, too, sometimes at least half of what the big places charge. Best of all, you personally know who is taking care of mom or dad. When you interview the owner, it is much easier to glean impressions than if you interview a large facility's marketing manager—who will not be looking after your mother.

Many of these care homes, especially the good ones, stay fully occupied. That is why proactive decision-making to act early on the part of the family is so important. See additional remarks about proactive planning later in this chapter.

Family Support

As more of us live longer and have limited financial means to pay for fancy senior facilities over a prolonged period, we will see more integrated families in which three—or four—generations of family live together. This is not necessarily bad. I have seen support from family members extend the life and wellbeing of many seniors. Yes, family complications exist between in-laws, blended families, and life schedules. But combining incomes and expenses among household members enhances care for elder loved ones and provides more social interaction, each found to be important in extending a productive life and slowing the onset of symptoms of dementia.

One of the sad ironies of grandparents living the good life in often distant retirement communities is the isolation from other family members that often results. Geographic and social distance between generations often make transitions for the senior difficult to manage, particularly if he or she has no companion to provide help.

As the grandparent develops more intensive care needs, the live-in family may still need to resort to outside professional help. Such assistance may include bathroom duties, physical therapy, and attendant duties while the rest of the family is out of the house. Cost for the services is usually borne by the family, unless specific medical and nursing care qualify for Medicaid or Medicare.

Transition Realities

As I outlined earlier, most seniors will go through an almost predictable path of retirement, slow-down, and then decline. During this process there are a whole series of decisions to make, planning to do, and emotions to deal with that make the path anything but predictable, especially for the family trying to help mom or dad through it all.

Here is just a short list of factors that I have witnessed which complicate matters and make life miserable and stressful for everyone involved near the end of the twilight years.

1. The senior may be inflexible with their living arrangements, perhaps wishing to stay independent in their home or residence far too long and continuing to drive when they are not able to safely. These are the same people who, even after having several falls, think they do not need to wear a life alert or special phone to notify medical help if in distress.

2. Children or other support people may jointly be connected to the elder by marriage or birth, but do not get along with each other. The number of siblings I see who are not on good terms and do not help each other astounds me.

3. Children or other support people may be officially connected, such as by blood or marriage, to the senior, but do not get along with the senior, or vice versa. Many times, it is not the fault of the parent, but often it is. More often than not, it is difficult to tell whose fault it is, but past scars and poor communication make administering end-of-life planning a challenge.

4. The senior may have a caregiver who is a crook. Often, well-to-do elders who live alone—and who are determined to stay in their independent residence—will hire senior care service or other individuals to come to the house and care for them, to do chores, cooking, driving, and to keep company. This usually works out OK, but I have also witnessed cases where the attendant manipulates and steals from the person they are supposed to be caring for. I have no statistics, but it appears this happens most frequently with elder widowers being cared for by a hired female, usually in her forties. It is an almost uncanny pattern in which a lonely man, perhaps recently widowed, becomes infatuated beyond reason when a new

woman comes into the house and lavishes him with attention and smiles. My case files include examples of bank account depletion, extravagant spending on the attendant, and even a suspected murder when the old man's money ran out.

5. The senior or the family may be overly concerned about the money running out, or heirs missing out on expected inheritance. In many cases, this is a legitimate concern; in others it should not be, but is. As a result, the living situation of our elder is not properly addressed. Perhaps the senior would do better with home health care, or on the other hand, a move into a senior living facility.

Believe it or not, it's not family members who are most guilty of being penny wise and pound foolish. Too often seniors themselves stubbornly refuse to pay for services they need to make their lives safer and healthier. I've seen a millionaire keep his home as hot as a greenhouse to save on electricity, and another retiree spend lavishly on their children but cry poor when I suggested a $20 monthly cost for a life alert system.

I tell many of my clients who have sufficient savings that they have reached the point in their lives where their decisions should be less based on financial considerations and more on health or lifestyle. It's a hard sell.

6. The family may live too far away to keep an eye on their loved one or to be an attentive healthcare advocate in time of need. When Grandma is falling at home twice a week, ending up in the hospital for heart problems, or can't remember if she paid her property taxes or not, she needs help. At first, the children—and Grandma—believe they can handle things over the phone and with a few visits. As health issues intensify, administering long distance assistance becomes difficult, if not impossible.

The biggest problem often occurs in dealing with the medical community. The elder is not always able to understand her doctor's instructions, implement recommendations, or even remember what they said. Then there are the stays in hospitals or rehabilitation centers. Caregivers at these places do the best they can, but let's face it, many are overworked, very busy with other patients, and may not give the care or attention that we hope our beloved family member would receive. Once in a while, the patient needs someone to go out into the hallway, call for a nurse, or raise a little hell to get needed help. If the family is 1,200 miles away, such hands-on assistance is impossible.

---

7. The gray areas of dementia and legal competency are insidious. Unfortunately, we are not doing the New York Times crossword puzzle one day and struggling to remember the names of our children the next. Dementia, a catch-all term that describes symptoms of memory loss, impaired reasoning, or personality change, has many causes including Alzheimer's disease, hardening of carotid arteries, and brain injuries. For those who suffer it, symptoms come on gradually over a long period. Spouses may make fun excuses for their mate's changing behavior; other family members may not even notice a transition occurring. People in my profession can pick it up pretty quickly because we immediately notice that old Joe cannot recall details about his portfolio as in the past. For Joe to have an understanding and patient spouse or family member nearby to help is a luxury when such symptoms begin to appear.

Proactive Planning is the Key

The most successful clients that transition through the evolution of retirement as outlined earlier in this chapter do so because they attempt to realistically assess their future. When we boil it all down, there are two primary parties: the elder and the family of the elder. Each party must participate in this planning process. Typically, and not always ideally, the party with the controlling finances exerts the largest control.

Thus, if Grandpa has lots of money and he is determined to stay in his golf club community home until he drops dead, very little planning will be done, and only after he is malnourished, very weak, and has had several falling incidents in which no one discovered him until after two days have passed, will he even consider changing his living arrangement. Maybe.

On the other hand, if adult children are financially comfortable, they often control the process for their parents. The kids are able to influence where the retiree moves, in what type of place he lives, and perhaps invite him to move in with one of them.

Probably the most important part of planning is to be realistic. Realize that you may not be able, or even desire, to maintain your own home forever. Realize that if your spouse dies, it will be lonely and there will be no one to eat with, so you will eat less, and less nutritionally. Realize that you will need your children or other close relatives to be there with you in the hospital to talk to doctors and to be your healthcare advocate. And realize that your loved ones will not be able to give you the kind of help you will need—and that they desperately want to give—if you live five states away from them.

Clients of mine who plan for their transitions and do something about it—in advance—are generally the happiest and less stressed. And their kids are very much less stressed as well.

Specific Recommendations

Buy Insurance - Of course, having long-term care insurance, whether through a traditional policy or through a convertible life policy, should be on the planning table. In many cases, by the time this is considered, the insurability of the policy owner or the cost may be prohibitive. Indeed, most retirees have no long-term care insurance, even though, and I'll repeat it again, 70% of us will need long-term care, a higher probability than having to use our homeowners insurance for a major expense.

Plan to live close to family - at some point: When I relocated to Florida from Pennsylvania, my father followed soon after. He told me that a primary motivation for him was to be near *me* as he aged so that he would not be a long distance inconvenience. I smiled incredulously, but as the years rolled by, his wisdom became evident. My father eventually suffered from dementia and fell victim to cancer. I was there with him every step of the way.

I am not asking every retiree to immediately pack a bag to relocate to their daughter's basement. I am asking you to keep this option in mind—for some eventual time—and to talk to your kids about it. Perhaps they'll have supportive ideas of their own. Who knows, maybe they have future plans to move closer to *you.*

Check out senior living facilities—now - With very few exceptions, my happiest and healthiest senior clients are those who moved to a senior care facility proactively, that is, before it was too late. Too late means before you start to fall, or become socially isolated, or before your primary meals are frozen TV dinners. And too late also means transitioning on time so you can enjoy the stress-free comfortable lifestyle many of these places offer.

Senior facilities ain't what they used to be. We're not just talking about nursing homes here or tired apartment buildings. Communities that cater to aging seniors are often like country clubs or luxurious hotels. The classification of living units offered for those who can plan and afford it go from fully independent living, to assisted living, to perhaps memory units, then finally to full nursing care. What's more, larger complexes and companies may offer all of these on one campus, sort of a one-stop shopping for senior living.

Retirees benefit from these facilities because they usually feed you, socialize you, and to varying degrees, watch over you. It is very doubtful that you will fall in your apartment and go undiscovered for several days, as I have seen with people living in their traditional home. Review and compare price structures of different places. Some of them have pricing and deposit packages complex enough to make assistance from a financial professional (CPA, financial planner) advisable. My senior clients who go into these places before they're too old call them stress-free luxury apartment-living. The most attractive communities may have a waiting list, so advance planning is a must. And most important: Make sure you like the food!

The selected senior facility does not have to be part of a 50-acre complex. It can be a small home-like facility or a move-in with the kids. I know more and more clients who are building a grandma suite in the backyard of their children's home.

Talk With Family

Of course, the grandma suite is an excellent segue to talk about family communications. Planning and building a new addition to a house requires lots of it. Ideally, by the age of 70, but certainly no later than 75, whether married or not, there should be a serious conversation about resources and goals and how the family is going to eventually take care of each other. Such conversations are difficult enough with *blood* families; with blended families it's downright challenging. This is an ideal time to have an elder family attorney or financial planner sit in to offer suggestions—or to mediate contentious issues. Unfortunately, as stated in the estate planning chapter, a written will can be applied to Grandma only *after* she is deceased, not while she is lying unconscious in a hospital bed. Moreover, most revocable trusts do not include, but can and should, more planning provisions related to elder care. As a result, I advise many seniors, with the help of their family, to devise a plan outline of how they see the path to skilled nursing (home) care, just in case it's needed.

Components of the plan may include:

1. Determination of monthly funds available to care for mom (and or dad). (*How much can we afford will determine lifestyle options*)
2. Identification of close friends and neighbors who will "look over" the senior as they age.
3. Discussion of preference for evolution and timing of transitional moves. (*Where's dad going to be living 10 years from now so it's best for everyone?)*
4. Identification of which family members, because of physical or social closeness, are to be the point people and healthcare advocates. (*Should mom eventually move closer to daughter Kathy because Kathy is a registered nurse?)*

Get the planning done, then you can enjoy the rest of your life.

Three Critical Takeaways from Chapter

1. The evolution of aging is predictable.
2. For family and seniors, nothing seems predictable.
3. Proactive planning and flexibility are paramount.

Part Four

WRAP UP

Chapter 19

You Can Do It!

In this short book I have attempted to cover the basics of key financial elements that affect virtually all our lives. All of us should have at least a cursory knowledge of these matters. I am fully aware that each chapter's topic has consumed numerous books as a stand-alone subject. However, I hope that you can now have a working knowledge to better navigate our complex society. We've discussed things like how to save money, how much we need to save, life insurance, the basics of our crazy income tax system, and considerations for old-age planning. Finally, we can't forget the chapter on marriage advice—not how to survive it, but rather some financial considerations of even doing it in the first place.

When you come right down to it, it's all about not just financially managing current affairs, but really planning for the future—some distant abstract time in which we may or may not even exist. As I said in the introduction, it is a quest for eventual freedom—yes, to be free of debt and stress, but also to have the freedom to live life as you wish.

Over the years I've tried to understand why some people are better about planning for the future than others. I've come to believe that the key to success is not intelligence or the type of job one has, or even the amount of money one may be lucky enough to earn. It is certainly not based on the level of education; some of the best planners and savers I've worked with barely finished high school. Some of the worst planners have been high-income doctors.

No, I believe that good planners for the future are ones who *believe* in their future. Yes, they may have a healthy fear that they don't want to be broke 20 years from now, but more, there's an underlying optimism—a belief—that there *will* be a 20-years from now for them to be around for. This may sound obviously basic and foreign to many of you, but I've met several people who do not, and, in their own minds, cannot believe or worry about 20 years, or even 20 months, into the future.

Perhaps because of a rough childhood, inadequate family support, or other insecurities, there is a deep set feeling they cannot have a belief in the future. As a result, the poor planners have an instilled feeling that they should enjoy what they can now, and spend what they can now, and not save a dime of it, because it may be all gone tomorrow, anyway. *Grab all the gusto you can today*. On the surface, it appears to be an attitude of irresponsibility, but I view it differently. I think there is an underlying sentiment of pessimism. And this pessimism is a major component that prevents their putting enough into their 401(k), or contributing to an IRA, or having a savings account.

So, if you've been a poor saver, ask yourself why. Have a heart-to-heart with yourself. Persuade yourself to be more optimistic about *you*—and about the fact that you will probably be around for a long time. In fact, at least 70% of you will make it to age 65. And 30% will make it to age 90. You really can't bet against those odds.

In short, enjoy life, but plan for a long one.

When planning for your life and your finances, get a partner or mentor to help you, and probably more than one. Relatives and friends are good motivators, but often are dead wrong about complex issues. Seek professional help. Yes, they charge a fee, but if they're good, their accumulated wisdom and technical knowledge can be useful for you.

It has been my observation over the years that, ironically, those who seek planning advice are probably those who least need it. At the same time, those who really need help, rarely seek it. College counselors say it is the same with students: those who need the advice never show up in their offices.

For legal advice, see an attorney. An hour's consultation that costs a few hundred dollars can easily save thousands later, whether it is a real estate transaction, starting a new business or a new marriage.

For financial advice, seek someone who is not going to profit based on the advice they give. A person who sells annuities will probably recommend that you buy an annuity.

Warren Buffett says it best: "Never ask a barber if you need a haircut."

Other financial advisors come in a cereal bowl of alphabet credentials and fee structures that confuse everyone. Some of them work on commissions, some work on charging hourly fees, and some work on the amount of assets they manage for you. And still others work on a combination of all of the above.

One type of financial advisor is called a Registered Investment Advisor (RIA). Such professionals are held to a higher standard by regulators in that they must act as your fiduciary when managing your assets. That is, they must put your interest before their own. If they don't, you can sue them, or worse, report them to authorities. Try to find a fee-only RIA so you know there can be no hidden commission or compensation motives.

When you visit a professional, check out their website beforehand, ask those you know if they've worked with his or her firm, and when you go for your initial appointment, take a friend or loved one so they can size up the advisor, too.

Warren Buffett has lots of great quotes, but one of his best was in response to a question regarding to what he owes his success. His reply: "My wealth has come from a combination of living in America, some lucky genes, and compound interest."

His positive spirit about the country and his life has always been an unwavering inspiration for all of us.

Now it is your turn. Go out there and plan a great life. And never lose your optimism.

You can do it!

About the Author

J. A. Dougherty, (MBA, New York University; B.S., LaSalle University), CPA, RIA, has been involved with helping clients wade through complexities of investments, taxes, and retirement planning for more than 30 years. Before relocating to Spring Hill, Florida, he worked as a senior financial analyst for a Fortune 500 tech company and then with an international consulting firm advising large corporations on various cost and organizational issues. Dougherty has lectured on tax and estate planning matters and hosted a radio advice show.

He is also author of *Unconditional Love Sucks: How an Old Myth Ruins Relationships*, about managing romantic relationships to achieve financial and personal success.

Dougherty & Associates, LLC
4048 Deltona Blvd.
Spring Hill, FL 34606
352.238.6411

www.DoughertyInvestments.com

Thank You Notes

This book was made possible—and certainly better—because several people dedicated their valuable time, effort and talents to make it better.

Michael Angier serves as my helmsman and navigator once again, instrumental in design, format, and getting this thing published. He is an accomplished author and consultant, and without his assistance and presence, I probably would not have bothered to undertake this project.

Several people contributed eagle-eye editing and proofing as well as ideas for title and structure. I may be missing a few, but Ivan Abernathy, Robert Shuleit, and Nicholette Hamel offered much in this regard. Through his extensive experience and smarts in the industry, Randall Bowser provided much assistance with the chapter on auto purchases. Dr. Robert Schneider deserves special thanks for bringing to this project his extensive effort, editorial experience, and wide knowledge on the subject matter. Thanks much.

Don and Harriet Neill live a thousand miles away but their connection to this effort is incomparably close. Their detailed proofing, formatting, editing, and even paragraph rewrites have provided a polish and finish to this book for which I shall be forever grateful.

As I've stated in a previous publication, I cannot forget to thank my clients. Over the years, so many have become close friends and companions. Their financial adventures have provided wisdom for us all. During the journey of their lives and mine, I have enjoyed sharing the ride.

Of course, a perennial thank-you to sons, Seann and Ryan Dougherty, Steven Head, sister, Katherine Stahl, and to my incredible, loving, patient, and understanding wife, Susan. Finally, my parents Jack and Dolores may be gone from this earth, but their influence and example can never be forgotten—it is really to them that so many thanks are due.

Made in United States
Troutdale, OR
08/22/2024

22229250R00110